OVERVIEW

Overview

Do you know how to write and present an effective business case that can get you the resources you need for a new project? Organizational budgets for new projects are typically very tight. Without a written business case, you have little chance of persuading decision makers within your organization to implement your new project idea over a competing idea.

A business case contains information about a proposed project. It outlines the best way to deal with a problem or an opportunity that is facing your company. The business case is the tool that you use to obtain the resources for the project.

In this book, you'll learn the information you'll need to successfully present a business case. This book will provide you with step-by-step instructions on researching and presenting the components of your case. You'll also find out how to tailor your case to a specific audience.

Do you know what a business case is, and what it can do for you? A business case is a document containing all of the information necessary for an individual, group, or organization to evaluate a proposed project.

A good business case enables you to secure the resources and capital investment you need to implement your project. The most obvious reason for putting together a business case is to persuade your organization to invest in a new project. However, a business case is not just a financial document.

While all business cases should include financial justification, this should not be the only purpose of the business-case document. The business case should be where all relevant facts are documented and linked together. Jan is a finance manager for an architectural firm. She's working on an initiative for an improved payroll plan for the company.

Her business case describes the shortcomings of the current payroll system, and explains how her solution can increase efficiency and save the organization both time and money.

It also details the resources needed to deliver the solution. A good business case should tell its audience:

- why the project is needed,
- how it will create solutions to the issues and opportunities facing the organization,
- what will happen to the business if the project is not undertaken,
- when the project will be deployed,
- how much capital investment, human resources, and time will be needed to deliver the project.

Organizational budgets for new projects are often very tight, so competition for resources is high among managers and project leaders. Without a written business case, you have very little chance of persuading decision makers within your organization to implement your proposed project over a competing project.

It's worth taking the time to produce a good business case for your project, as it can help you to secure the project resources you need. This book will provide you with the information you need to write a business case. You will learn what a business case is, and when one is used. You'll find out what you need to do before you start writing a business case, and what information should be included in your business case.

You'll also receive instructions on researching and presenting your business case, and how to tailor it to a specific audience.

Are you confident that you could deliver a winning business case presentation to a room full of people? Would you know how to prepare your presentation to ensure it has a cohesive structure and will be easy for your audience to follow?

Delivering a high-quality business case presentation is not an easy thing to do. By analyzing your audience, developing effective preparation techniques, and using visual aids persuasively, you will maximize your chances of delivering a first-class business case presentation.

Jane is disappointed with a recent business case presentation that she gave to a group of senior managers at her client's head office. She talks to her supervisor,

John, about some of the main difficulties she had with her presentation. She identifies three important problems.

The room was larger than she expected. She was concerned that her audience had difficulty hearing her voice. The overhead projector was different to the one she was used to, and there was a delay as she tried to load some slides. Toward the end of the presentation, one of the managers asked her a question that she found difficult to answer.

The more you learn about what is required to make a good business case presentation, the more confident you will be when making your next presentation. In this book, you will learn how to practice and rehearse your presentation, control your environment, establish a rapport with your audience, and apply a strong closing to your business case presentation.

CHAPTER 1 - PREPARING A BUSINESS CASE

SECTION 1 - INTRODUCTION TO BUSINESS CASES

SECTION 1 - Introduction to Business Cases

In this topic, you have learned about the purpose of business cases and when they are used. A business case is used to present the business issue and define the scope of the business issue. It presents options. The case is used to seek approval for the preferred option to be pursued as a project. It helps to obtain human, physical, and financial resources for a project. It documents what the project will accomplish and what the benefits will be.

A business case is used during all stages of a project's life cycle. It is used to obtain funding, it is referred to during the project life cycle, and it is used after a project is finished to assess what the project has delivered.

In this topic, you have seen how corporate culture affects business cases. There is no one correct way of presenting a business case, and the organization's business culture is important in this respect. Corporate culture determines the length and the format of the business case, who initiates the business case, the development process and life cycle, and how it will be presented and processed in the organization.

WRITING A GOOD BUSINESS CASE

Writing a good business case

A 1995 survey by the Standish Group found that, in IT, more than 83% of all project investments fail to meet their economic goals. A well-planned business case can make the members of your organization aware of impending problems or opportunities.

An effective business case can secure the resources you need to get your project off the ground. Securing the resources for a project can be the first step toward achieving goals that benefit your company and your career. A good business case is an asset in all stages of a project's life cycle.

It is used for:

getting the financial support

At the initial stages, the business case can be instrumental in obtaining the necessary funding and resources.

explaining project benefits

A business case explains benefits and gets support of end users.

keeping the project focused on the original plan

When the project is in development, the business case keeps the project focused on the original plan.

getting continuous executive support

The business case can get continuous executive support. This provides the moral support and conceptual support required to sustain a project.

serving as the foundation of a feedback loop for measuring value-creation progress

If elements of the project do not conform to what is outlined in the business case, they can be modified as soon as the discrepancy between the work in progress and the outcome required by the business case is spotted.

Question

Identify the benefits of writing an effective business case.

Options:

1. It can secure the resources required to develop the project
2. It can explain the benefits and get support for the concept
3. The business case keeps the project focused on the original plan
4. It can be used as a press release
5. It serves as a standard to determine the progress of the project at each stage in its development

Answer:

Option 1: This option is correct. A well-written business case can secure the funding and resources required for a project.

Option 2: This option is correct. A well-written business plan can provide an overview of an upcoming project.

Option 3: This option is correct. The business case document can help to keep everyone focused on the goals of the project.

Option 4: This option is incorrect. The business case can help to outline the reason for starting a project and to obtain the necessary resources, but it is not intended as a marketing document.

Option 5: This option is correct. The business case states the project's aims and can be used to ensure that the project stays on track.

A business case can make the members of your organization aware of impending problems or opportunities and it can secure the resources necessary to get a project off the ground. A good business case is an asset in all stages of a project's life cycle. This lesson will examine how corporate culture influences the development of business cases.

DEVELOPING A BUSINESS CASE

Developing a business case

A business case is a document that presents a comprehensive view of the project and provides the financial justification for implementation. It is a critical component of your project because it makes the case for change and provides the financial justification for a project.

Project teams prepare business cases for a number of reasons. A business case is mainly developed to

- present the business issue - it should identify the business need or opportunity and explain why the issue needs to be addressed,
- define the scope of the business issue - it should present an analysis of the costs, benefits, and risks associated with the project,
- present options and make recommendations as to the most appropriate option and detail the resources necessary to undertake this book of action,

- seek approval for the preferred option to be pursued as a project,
- obtain human, physical, and financial resources,
- document what the project will accomplish and what the benefits will be, including the deliverables.

The business case is a useful tool throughout a project's life cycle.

It is particularly useful:

when the project is approved to proceed and be funded

When the project is approved, the business case is then used as the key input into the project's detailed planning stages, and it communicates to the project manager and project team members what approved outcomes must be achieved.

during the project's implementation stages

During the implementation stages, the business case is used by the project manager to regularly test that the project is progressing as approved. It also is used to determine whether any key assumptions or objectives have changed and whether the business case needs reassessing.

once a project has been completed

When the project has been completed, the business case is used to compare what has actually been delivered to the business with what was approved in the business case.

Maria, a process engineer for a healthcare company, believes that the most critical need in the organization is to reduce the number of defects in diagnostic detection kits that the company is currently producing.

She is developing a business case that examines a number of ways to improve the quality procedures in the manufacturing plant. The business case analyzes the costs, benefits, and risks associated with each option and recommends that a new design inspection program should be introduced.

The business case explains how the inspection program will eliminate defects early on in the manufacturing process and save rework time. It estimates how long the program will take to implement and the savings that will be made. It details the commitment necessary to introduce the program in terms of time, money, and human resources.

Question

A business case serves many purposes.

Why would you develop a business case for a project?

Options:

1. To understand the value of your project in today's business environment
2. To present the business issue
3. To define the scope of the business issue
4. To present options and make recommendations
5. To seek conceptual approval for the project
6. To obtain human, physical, and financial resources for a project
7. To document what the project will accomplish and what the benefits will be

Answer:

Option 1: This option is incorrect. The business case is intended to raise awareness of a problem or opportunity that is facing your company.

Option 2: This option is correct. The business case allows you to raise the issue of the particular problem or opportunity that the business is facing.

Option 3: This option is correct. The extent of the problem or the opportunities that may be available are defined in the business case.

Option 4: This option is correct. The business case should lay out a suitable plan of action to address the issues that the company faces.

Option 5: This option is correct. You would use a business case to gain approval from management to proceed with a new project.

Option 6: This option is correct. A business case outlines the resources that are required to begin a new project.

Option 7: This option is correct. This information can prove to be the deciding factor in getting approval for your project.

FEATURES OF A BUSINESS CASE

Features of a business case

There is no one correct way of presenting a business case. Each business case will inevitably have a significant degree of subjectivity associated with it. That subjectivity often arises from an organization's business culture.

Corporate culture can influence a business case in many ways:

- it determines the length and the format of a business case,
- it influences who initiates the business case and how it will be presented,
- it influences the development process and life cycle and how the project will be presented and processed in the organization.

How does corporate culture determine the length and format of the business case? John works for a small, family-run firm and his boss is interested in descriptions of how a new computer- based business process will change the way things are done. His boss does not require these benefits to be quantified in detail.

David works for a large, multinational company that is steeped in bureaucracy. His employers require detailed financial projections for every project that he proposes. The differences in the corporate cultures will affect the length and format of the business cases that John and David are preparing. David will have to include a lot of detailed financial information in his business case, thereby increasing the overall length.

Corporate culture also determines who initiates the business case.

For example, Meg works in a manufacturing plant where top management determines the business case and it is handed down to more junior staff for development.

She has been asked to design an inspection program to eliminate manufacturing defects early in a process and help save considerable time. Tim works in a software development company. He is a team lead in the Marketing Department and believes there may be a demand for the company's products in overseas markets.

He draws up a business case to raise the possibility of translating the software to other languages.

The different approaches reflect the difference in culture in the companies. In Meg's company, new projects are thought up by management. Tim's company, in contrast, allows staff at all levels to propose new projects. Corporate culture determines the development process and life cycle of a business case. For example, Loretta, an executive, manages Imagenie, a small, privately owned company.

When the head of a department wishes to develop a business case he uses a template. Filling out the template provides all of the information required for the proposed project. The completed business case is then reviewed and revised by members of the department in question before it is presented to Loretta for approval.

The business case development process can be very different, however, in larger organizations.

For example, when federal agencies present business cases, the process requires agencies to answer hundreds of questions covering five life cycle phases, IT and non-IT investments, and infrastructure and consolidation investments. Then agencies are required to fit their business rationale into a single template - the Exhibit 300.

Therefore, the bigger the company, the greater the structure and formality required in the development process and life cycle. Small companies can use a less formal development process. The way in which a business case is presented will depend very much on the corporate culture in which it was developed.

Here are examples of how some business cases were presented:

online

Emily's company is considering expanding its delivery of web-based services. A business plan is prepared and delivered over the web. This method of presentation is designed to underline the ability of existing web technology to deliver the proposed new services that the company intends to supply.

informal company meeting

Stan works for a small company that is considering expanding its direct marketing division. The head of the sales team makes the presentation directly to the company owner in his office, so that questions can be answered and issues expanded upon as needed.

formal conference

Linda is in charge of a department in a large multinational company. Her business case is presented in a very formal manner to a number of high-level executives, industry analysts, and investment bankers.

In smaller companies, the business case may simply be reviewed by managers who then decide whether resources will be allocated to the project.

Question

Identify the factors involved in the development of a business case that are influenced by corporate culture.

Options:

1. The length and format of the business case
2. The way in which it is processed in the organization
3. The purpose of a business case
4. The way in which it is presented
5. The development process and life cycle of the business case
6. The persons involved in initiating the business case

Answer:

Option 1: This option is correct. Some companies will require detailed information about all aspects of a new project and how they will affect the existing business model.

Other companies will only require a brief outline of the project and its expected benefits.

Option 2: This option is correct. The business case may result in new departments being created and new procedures being set up, or it may result in the once-off expenditure on new workplace equipment.

Option 3: This option is incorrect. A business case always has the same function: to obtain the resources necessary to implement a new project.

Option 4: This option is correct. The presentation of a business case can vary widely from company to company. It can be a relatively informal affair, where it is almost at the level of a conversation.

Alternatively, it could be a formal presentation to upper management, or it could take advantage of specialist technologies as a means of demonstrating the value of those technologies.

Option 5: This option is correct. The development and life cycle of a business case are influenced by the amount of detail required by the departments that will have a say in approving or providing resources for the project.

Option 6: This option is correct. In some cases, a company's high-level management decides on a possible business case and asks a junior member of staff or a department to research it.

In other cases, it may happen that any member of staff in a company can prepare a business case when they become aware of a problem or opportunity facing the company.

x

SECTION 2 - PLANNING A BUSINESS CASE

SECTION 2 - Planning a Business Case

You must carry out proper research before you begin writing a business case. Carrying out research will give you in-depth knowledge of the resources required to implement a new project that will capitalize on a problem or opportunity that is facing the company. This will allow you to define the scope of your business case.

This topic will examine the factors that are taken into account when defining the scope of a business case, and will help you to decide on the scope of a business case.

The scope of a business case is determined by a number of factors - business case drivers and boundaries, the deliverables, project teams, and the schedule. Defining the scope of a business case before you start to write the business case helps to identify needed resources, avoid time-wasting detours, and accurately set management expectation.

Assumptions and constraints relating to a project must be taken into account when preparing a business case.

This topic examined the factors involved in determining the scope of a business case and outlined the benefits to doing so.

This topic identified the costs that should be considered when preparing a business case and examined the techniques and benefits involved in creating a business case. There are a number of techniques used to calculate financial ratios in cost-benefit analysis: 1) the payback, 2) the return on investment (ROI), 3) the net present value (NPV), and 4) the internal rate of return (IRR).

There are two generic categories of benefit - tangible and intangible. These can be further categorized as quantifiable or unquantifiable. It is generally believed that cost-benefit analysis provides hard (tangible and quantifiable) measures of a company's financial performance over a period of time, while the other measures are soft (difficult to quantify and measure).

In this topic you have learned the benefits of correctly identifying the decision makers of a business case, and the methods you should use to convince decision makers about the feasibility of a project. You have been introduced to the factors (both tangible and intangible) used by decision makers to determine the attractiveness of investment alternatives.

RESEARCH YOUR BUSINESS CASE

Research your business case

"Plans get you into things, but you got to work your way out." – Will Rogers

What happens when you do not conduct effective research? If you have carried out thorough research for a business case, you will be aware of the options available to your company to capitalize on opportunities or deal with problems. A business case increases the chances of success of a project.

You will know the resources that will be required to implement the new project.

You will be familiar with the business concerns of your company's owners and management, and can focus a business case presentation on an area of concern. The business case is useful for generating information that you will need in order to answer questions that may arise.

Question

Select the benefits of researching a business case.

Options:

1. You will have an in-depth knowledge of the resources that will be required to implement a new project

2. Your business case is guaranteed to be successful

3. You will be aware of the options available to your company to capitalize on opportunities or deal with problems

4. You will be better able to focus a business case presentation on an area of concern to owners and management

Answer:

Option 1: This option is correct. You can present a business case, confident in the knowledge that you are fully aware of all the resources required for the project.

Option 2: This option is incorrect. Research on its own doesn't guarantee that a business case will be successful, but it will significantly increase its chances.

Option 3: This option is correct. Conducting proper research will make you aware of the problems and opportunities facing your company.

Option 4: This option is correct. Your business case has more chance of being successful if it deals with issues that are of concern to the decision makers in your company.

x

BENEFITS OF DEFINING THE SCOPE

Benefits of defining the scope

Scope determines the size of a project. A business case scope defines the boundaries of the proposed project and states them clearly for the audience and decision makers.

Determining the scope of a project involves discussions with clients and users of project deliverables to determine their requirements and needs.

Successful business enterprises consider seven factors when determining whether to develop a new product or service. These factors should be considered at the planning stages of a case:

the business concept

New business concepts generally attempt to develop something new, something better, a new or under-served market, or greater integration of a company's products or services.

business focus

Staying focused on the central character of the business will help ensure that any new ideas that are developed are aligned with the corporate strategy. The mission statement can help managers remain focused.

management

A project is more likely to succeed if the managers possess certain attributes: industry or management experience, a realistic approach to business needs, a flexible attitude to change, and the ability to work well with other people.

industry health

The economic health of an industry is a strong indicator of whether a product will be successful. There is an increased chance that a new product or service will be successful if it responds to a healthy industry.

the market

Key market factors that affect the product success include market readiness, demographics, the size of the market area, and pricing.

financial control

Financial control requires establishing the profit margins for a project and includes correctly estimating costs, such as research and marketing, having access to financial information, and managing cash flow.

anticipation of change

It is important to anticipate changes that may affect the new project. These include technology changes, social changes, and new projects introduced by rivals.

Question

Identify the factors that should be considered at the planning stages of a business case.

Options:

1. The business concept
2. Business focus

3. Management
4. Industry health
5. Presentation format
6. The market
7. Financial control
8. Anticipation of change

Answer:

Option 1: This option is correct. A business concept is an attempt to develop a new or improved product or service.

Option 2: This option is correct. New projects have a better chance of success if they are aligned with the organization's stated corporate strategy.

Option 3: This option is correct. It is important to select the right managers for a new project. Option 4: This option is correct. A new project is more likely to succeed if it is developed as part of a strong and healthy industry.

Option 5: This option is incorrect. The format used to present the business case is not relevant to defining the scope of the project.

Option 6: This option is correct. If a project involves creating a new product, that product is more likely to be successful if certain market factors have been taken into account. The factors include market readiness, demographics, the size of the market area, and pricing.

Option 7: This option is correct. All the financial aspects of the proposed project should be taken into account at the planning stages of the business case.

Option 8: This option is correct. It is important to anticipate changes that may affect the new product or service and take these into account when developing the business case.

To increase the chances of securing funding for your project, your business case must have:

- agreement among the project team on the objectives of the project,
- a controlled scope, to ensure that everyone involved understands exactly what can be accomplished within a given time frame and budget,
- a work plan that shows an overall path for the development of the project and what is necessary to achieve it,
- constant, effective communication among everyone involved in the project in order to coordinate action, recognize and solve problems, and react to changes.

The scope defines the size of a project. It has a large impact on the probability of project success. In general, smaller projects are more manageable and therefore have a higher likelihood of success.

Scope can include such areas as project:

- Deliverables,
- Schedule,
- Features,
- Functions,
- Team,
- Resources,
- Standards and guidelines.

An item that is in scope will be included in the project--for example, a new computer system as part of a project to update a company's Order Processing Department.

Something deferred will be delivered in a later stage. Something out-of-scope will not be included in the project. It's important to explicitly identify items to be excluded from the scope to reduce misunderstandings and conflict.

Ralph and Marsha are managers in Gleeson Associates, a systems support company. They believe that the company should set up a training division and offer a range of books. Follow their conversation as they decide on the scope of the business case that they are going to prepare for the project.

Ralph: Hi Marsha. I have just been looking at the customer survey data. One area that consistently impressed customers was the high level of knowledge and expertise displayed by our staff.

Marsha: That's true. This expertise is a valuable resource and that's why the project to develop a Customer Training Department is such a good idea.

Ralph: Some staff training will be needed to get the department up and running.

Marsha: We will need to train the staff within the next three months so they will be ready for the official launch of our training books.

Ralph: I have an idea: if we are preparing a business case anyway to obtain funds and resources, could we expand the business case to obtain the funds we'll need to develop an Online Training Department?

Marsha: The Online Department is a good idea. However, it is outside the boundaries of this project, so we will not include it in this business case.

Ralph: You're right. It is outside the scope of the business case. Thanks for pointing that out.

The conversation Ralph and Marsha just had has enabled them to set the scope of the project. They have outlined the assumptions and constraints that will affect the project. And they are aware when project deliverables are outside the project scope.

The scope of a business case can be influenced by a number of factors:

- business case drivers,
- project constraints assumptions,
- user requirements and needs.

Business case drivers are the major business factors that propel the need for the project now, rather than six months ago or six months from now.

Identifying the primary business case drivers is extremely important and extra care must be taken to be sure the business drivers are correct. The drivers are specific to each project.

The correct drivers will:

- establish the direction of the business case,
- set the stage for the theme of the business case analysis,
- address issues of direct concern to senior management.

When preparing a business case, it's vital to identify all the project constraints as early as possible. A constraint is a restriction that will affect the performance of a project and limit activities throughout the project life cycle. Every project will have factors that limit or constrain its options.

For example, a predefined time frame to develop the project is a constraint that limits a project team's options regarding scope, staffing, and schedule. Another example of a constraint is a requirement that the product of a project be socially, economically, and environmentally sustainable.

It is unlikely that any project will have unlimited resources, funding, and time to complete the work. Constraints usually fall into three categories:

financial constraints

These limit the project team's options regarding the development of a business case and include such things as project costs, capital costs, materials, revenue, resource costs, and rate of return required.

time constraints

A time constraint, such as the establishment of imposed start and finish dates, or major milestones, limits team options by restricting the time permitted for delivering results.

quality constraints

These constraints affect specifications and standards to be achieved by the project. Regulations and standards imposed by the company or government are examples of quality constraints that influence the development of a business case.

Question

Ursula is preparing a business case to develop an information system for management and staff in the Marketing and Order Processing Division of her company.

Identify the constraints that will limit the options available for the business case that she will be preparing.

Options:

1. The order processing system must be developed in accordance with the strategic plan's development

infrastructure, methods, standards, and approved technology

2. The online system must increase the number of customer queries that are dealt with by 12% per month

3. The information system must be operational in one year

4. The information will contain details about the company's customers

5. The information system must achieve a 12% or better rate of return

Answer:

Option 1: This option is correct. Previous documents act as a constraint on a business case, and set the scope of a project.

Option 2: This option is correct. This is an example of a quality constraint that will affect the scope of the project.

Option 3: This option is correct. This is an example of a time constraint.

Option 4: This option is incorrect. This is outside the scope of the business case.

Option 5: This option is correct. This is one of the requirements that have been defined for the project, and as such it affects the scope of the business case.

Assumptions are factors that are considered to be true, real, or certain for planning purposes. It is essential that assumptions made are identified, validated, and recorded as part of preparing the business case.

Assumptions affect all aspects of the project. If an assumption is wrong it can be a risk to the project. Any assumptions as to the availability of specialist resources or skills should be identified here, and any dependencies that exist with other projects or initiatives should also be listed.

For example, if the date that a key person will become available is uncertain, a project manager might assume a specific start date. Such assumptions may or may not be accurate, and therefore involve a degree of risk.

The project team should understand the user requirements and what the customer needs. The team should meet with the customer to ensure that they have a common vision, and that the customer will have realistic expectations for the project.

Case Study: Question 1 of 4

Scenario

Evelyn is a project manager for Mailtronic, a small Internet insurance firm. Evelyn believes that the company should set up a Customer Support Department. Several customers have requested such a department and Evelyn believes that it could be a viable project.

Evelyn is now going to talk to members of her team to decide on the scope of the business case. Answer each question to help Evelyn decide on the scope of the business case.

Question

Identify which of the following considerations are within the scope of the business case that she will be preparing.

Options:

1. The department must be developed in accordance with the strategic plan's development infrastructure, methods, standards, and approved technology

2. The new department must increase the number of customer queries that are dealt with by 8% per month

3. The new department will make use of diagnostic software that is not yet created

4. If this project is successful and profitable, the team will use its improved standing in the company to develop a range of other projects

5. The department must be operational in three months

Answer:

Option 1: This option is correct. Previous documents act as a constraint on a business case, and set the scope of a project.

Option 2: This option is correct. This is an example of a quality constraint that will affect the scope of the project.

Option 3: This option is incorrect. This is outside the scope of the business case.

Option 4: This option is incorrect. The team must keep the focus on this project and not on any potential projects in the future.

Option 5: This option is correct. This is an example of a time constraint.

Case Study: Question 2 of 4

Evelyn talks to the company's Marketing Department. She tells them about the project and asks for their opinion. They responded positively, but said that it may be a good idea to expand the proposed project to include a survey that will help determine the insurance products that customers would like available.

How should Evelyn respond to their request?

Options:

1. She should expand the scope of the document to obtain the extra funds required for the requested product

2. She should tell the department that their request is outside of the scope of her project

3. She should ignore the request for the new product and she does not need to inform them that their request has not been included

Answer:

Option 1: This option is incorrect. The survey project is outside of the scope of the business case.

Option 2: This option is correct. Small projects are more manageable and have a higher chance of succeeding.

Option 3: This option is incorrect. Being upfront about the scope of the business case can help to avoid any future misunderstandings.

Case Study: Question 3 of 4

Evelyn has discussed the project with her team. They have drawn up a detailed financial projection for the expenditure required for the first three months of the project. Some members of the team feel that this information should not be included in the scope. Should Evelyn include it?

Options:

1. No
2. Yes

Answer:

Option 1: This option is incorrect. The scope should clearly state what the project will achieve and at what cost. Not including the information will mean that the scope is too vague to be meaningful.

Option 2: This option is correct because the scope should clearly state what can be accomplished within a specified time frame and budget. This information should be included so as to give the audience a clear idea of what will be achieved by the project.

Case Study: Question 4 of 4

Evelyn has been discussing the project with her team. A number of items have been discussed. Which issues will affect the scope of the business case?

Options:

1. The project must be up and running in three months
2. The staff required to set up the new department will be available as needed during the project life cycle
3. If this project is successful and is profitable, the team will use its improved standing in the company to develop a range of other projects
4. If Mailtronic does not set up a Customer Support Department, a rival company is poised to make such a move
5. The customers that the Marketing Department has talked to have indicated a preference for the availability of telephone and online customer support

Answer:

Option 1: This option is correct. This is an example of a time constraint.

Option 2: This option is correct. This is an assumption about the project and it affects the scope of the business case.

Option 3: This option is incorrect. This is outside the scope of the business case. It is a consideration that relates to the possible future projects, not to the project at hand.

Option 4: This option is correct. This is a business case driver, a business factor that propels the need for the project now, rather than six months ago or six months from now.

Option 5: This option is correct. This is an example of user needs and requirements, which affect the scope of a business case.

THE SCOPE OF A BUSINESS CASE

The scope of a business case

It has been said that front-end precision reduces back-end confusion.

It's important to lay the foundations for a successful business case by completing key front-end activities during the planning phase of the business case development. High-level decisions at the front end of business case development determine the project scope and direction.

Defining the scope of a business case before you actually begin to write the business case offers a number of benefits. Doing so helps you identify:

- the activities that will be required to undertake the project,
- what you will be able to accomplish in order to set accurate expectations for management,
- the project deliverables,
- needed resources,
- the project timeline.

If you have not carried out thorough research for a business case, you may not be aware of how to capitalize on opportunities or deal with problems within your organization.

You also may not know the resources that will be required to implement a new project.

Remember, defining the scope of a business case will enable you to focus your attention on the real area of concern, rather than spending time and energy on irrelevant details.

Question

Kevin works in a company that manufactures flavors for food products and medicines. He is preparing a business case to develop a new flavor.

Select the benefits of defining the project scope at the planning stage of the business case.

Options:

1. The expectations of management are aligned with content of the business case
2. The resources required to complete the project are identified
3. The project's deliverables are accurately described
4. The business case is guaranteed to be successful
5. Time-wasting activities that are not directly related to the project will be avoided
6. A realistic assessment of the project timescale will be obtained

Answer:

Option 1: This option is correct. Correctly defining the scope of the project ensures that managers will know what to expect when they read the business case.

Option 2: This option is correct. The resources that will be required are determined by the scope of the project.

Option 3: This option is correct. The project deliverables will become apparent when the scope of the project is defined.

Option 4: This option is incorrect. Defining the project scope at the planning stage has many advantages, but is not a magic formula that guarantees the success of a case.

Option 5: This option is correct. Defining the scope of a business case allows you to identify the activities required to undertake the project.

Option 6: This option is correct. A properly defined scope details the timescale for a project.

POTENTIAL BENEFIT TYPES OF A PROPOSED PROJECT

Potential benefit types of a proposed project

Business case costs

A business case usually contains a cost-benefit analysis because this is often a critical factor that upper management uses to decide whether a project is worth undertaking.

When preparing a business case, it is good practice to produce several different scenarios or financial pictures, such as best case, worst case, and most likely case, to assess costs.

It is also important to conduct "what-if" analysis, which shows what will happen if some of the assumptions are not realized. Here are some of the different costs that must be considered when developing a business case:

opportunity cost

Opportunity cost is the cost of something in terms of an untaken opportunity (and the benefits that could be received from that opportunity) or the most valuable alternative.

hidden costs

An unseen opportunity cost can become the hidden cost of that book of action. If there is no explicit monetary cost attached to a book of action, ignoring opportunity costs may produce the illusion that its benefits cost nothing at all.

marginal costs

Marginal costs are the costs of producing one more product or providing one more transaction.

time value of money

The time value of money is the value derived from the use of money over time. The present value is the value today of an amount that would exist in the future with a stated investment rate. Future value is the value in the future of a known amount today with a stated investment rate.

discounted cash flow

The discounted cash flow calculates the value of a future cash flow in terms of an equivalent value today. A future cash flow is discounted at some rate back to its present value so that all dollars, regardless of when collected, can be compared.

cost of capital

The cost of capital is the rate of return that is necessary to make a project viable. This includes the interest rate, which is the cost of borrowing money, and the hurdle rate. This is the minimum return on investment that a new product must exceed.

economic life

Economic life is the period of time during which an asset will have economic value and be usable.

terminal value

Terminal value is the value of an investment at the end of a period, taking into account a specified rate of interest. It is the value of a fully depreciated asset, such as a car or a computer at the end of its life.

Estimates for a project should include a number of costs:

- obtaining quotations from the different contributors to the project, such as suppliers, contractors, consultants, and outsourcers,
- calculating the cost of the development work,
- researching the cost of training staff.

It is important that you take all of the major costs of a project into consideration when preparing a business case.

For example, if you want to install a web-based ordering system in your company, it is vital that you include the cost of retraining staff and educating staff and customers in the costs. If you only include the cost of installing IT equipment, you could be underestimating the total cost of the project by a significant margin.

If a company is relocating, it is important that all costs are taken into consideration, not just the cost of the new building. Staff relocation costs, updating the company's address on all official literature, communications connections, and mail delivery will all need to be taken into consideration of and costed for.

Question

Match each of the costs that should be considered when preparing a business case with its definition.

Drag the letter beside each cost on the left to the corresponding box containing the definition on the right. Use each letter only once.

Options:

A. Opportunity cost
B. Hidden cost
C. Marginal cost
D. Cost of capital
E. Economic life
F. Terminal value

Targets:

1. This is the cost of something in terms of an untaken opportunity, or the most valuable alternative
2. An unseen opportunity cost
3. The cost of producing one more product or providing one more transaction
4. The rate of return that is necessary to make a project viable
5. The period of time during which an asset will have economic value and be usable
6. The value of an investment at the end of a period, taking into account a specified rate of interest

Answer:

This is the definition of opportunity cost. Money that is spent on one item is not available to spend on an alternate item. This is the definition of hidden cost.

An unseen opportunity cost can become the hidden cost of that book of action. If there is no explicit monetary cost attached to a book of action, ignoring opportunity costs may produce the illusion that its benefits cost nothing at all.

This is the definition of marginal cost.

This is the cost of creating an additional unit for a transaction. This is the definition of cost of capital.

This includes the interest rate, which is the cost of borrowing money, and the hurdle rate.

This is the minimum return on investment that a new product must exceed when it passes a particular phase of development.

This is the definition of economic life.

For example, this could refer to the lifespan of a piece of equipment used by a business. It could also refer to the length of time over which rent could be charged on a building

This is the definition of terminal value.

It is the value of a fully depreciated asset.

Calculating financial ratios

There are a number of techniques used to calculate financial ratios in cost-benefit analysis. Financial ratios are indicators of a firm's performance and financial situation. They are measures of capital, including debt to asset, current inventory, and debt to worth.

They are derived from the information in a company's financial statements. The debt to asset ratio is calculated by dividing the company's total liabilities by the total assets. The debt to worth ratio is calculated by dividing a company's total liabilities by the owners' equity (worth).

The current inventory is all the finished products that are ready for sale, but haven't been sold yet. The levels of these ratios, and the trends that they reveal over time, can be used to make inferences about a company's financial condition, its operations, and its attractiveness as an investment.

The following techniques are used when carrying out cost-benefit analysis:

Return On Investment (ROI)

The ROI is the ratio of net benefits to costs. The formula is (Benefits-Costs)/Costs.

Net Present Value (NPV)

The NPV is used to calculate and analyze the profitability of a project. The present value of cash inflow is subtracted from the sum of the discounted cash flows which are expected. NPV is used to analyze the profitability of an investment or project.

NPV compares the value of a sum of money today versus the value of that same sum of money in the future, after taking inflation and return into account. If the NPV of a prospective project is positive, then it should be accepted. If it is negative, then the project should be rejected.

Internal Rate of Return (IRR)

The IRR is the interest rate that makes net present value of all cash flow equal to zero. This is the return that a company would earn if it expanded or invested in itself, rather than investing elsewhere.

Question

Match the techniques used to calculate financial ratios with the information that they provide.

Drag each technique to its definition. Drag the letters on the left to the boxes on the right. Use each letter only once.

Options:

A. Net Present Value

B. Internal Rate of Return

C. Return On Investment

Targets:

1. This calculates the profitability of a project.

2. This is the interest rate that makes net present value of all cash flow equal to zero. 3. This is the ratio of net benefits to costs.

Answer:

This is the definition of Net Present Value. If the NPV of a prospective project is positive, then it should be accepted. If it is negative, then the project should be rejected.

This is the definition of Internal Rate of Return. This is the return that a company would earn if it expanded or invested in itself, rather than investing elsewhere.

This is the definition of Return On Investment. The formula is (Benefits-Costs)/Costs.

Potential project benefits

The value of a new project to an organization can be shown by listing its potential benefits in the business case. There are two generic categories of benefit: tangible and intangible.

You can do a number of things to help you estimate the potential benefits of a proposed project:

- interview executives and find out what they want,
- extract information from staff records to see what executives care about and what issues are important to them,
- talk to organizational neighbors to ascertain how the project will benefit them,
- follow the money chain to see where savings can be made,
- make sure that the project is effective and efficient -- this means that you will do the right thing and the do the thing right,

- interview stakeholders at their workplace.

A tangible benefit is a benefit produced by an investment that is immediately obvious and measurable. The term tangible benefit is usually used to refer to benefits that are directly reflected in the improvement in the profit performance of the organization.

Intangible benefits are benefits produced by an investment that are not immediately obvious or measurable. Benefits can be further classified as quantifiable or unquantifiable. A quantifiable benefit is one that can be measured. An unquantifiable benefit cannot be measured.

An increase in profits is an example of a quantifiable benefit. An increase in customer goodwill is an example of an unquantifiable benefit.

A quantifiable tangible benefit, for example, is one that directly affects the firm's profitability and the effect of which is such that it may be objectively measured. For example, it may be a reduction in costs or assets or an increase in revenue.

An unquantifiable tangible benefit can also be seen to directly affect the firm's profitability, but the precise extent to which it does cannot be directly measured.

For example, imagine your company's top management present a business case to introduce complex research information technology. An example of an unquantifiable tangible benefit here is the ability to obtain better information through the use of IT.

Intangible benefits can also be sub-classified in the same way. A quantifiable intangible benefit is one that can be measured, but its impact does not necessarily directly affect the firm's profitability. For example, installing research software would enable your company to obtain information faster.

Unquantifiable intangible benefits are benefits that cannot easily be measured and the impact of the benefit does not necessarily directly affect the firm's profitability. Examples include improved market reaction to the firm or potential employees' perception of the firm's product, or improved access to new staff.

Imagine a sales company has installed a new IT system. The system has reduced staff and increased the processing of orders and the speed of sharing information throughout the company. The benefits to the company fall into a number of different categories. What do you think they are?

First, the reduction in staff and assets and the increase in sales are examples of tangible and quantifiable benefits.

In addition, the quality of information flowing through the company has improved, so this is considered a corresponding tangible, albeit unquantifiable, benefit. The speed at which information can be transmitted and the improved staff morale due to greater efficiency are examples of intangible benefits, because they add to the company's profitability, but they are quantifiable.

The improved customer perception of the company's product is an example of an intangible and unquantifiable benefit.

Question

A company has installed a new database search facility. The new facility automates searches and simplifies data mining. The system has reduced staff, and increased the speed of information-sharing throughout the company.

Match the benefits with the class of benefit that they represent. Use each letter only once.

Options:

A. Reduction in costs and an increase in revenue

B. Better information

C. Faster information

D. Market reaction and access to new staff

Targets:

1. Tangible and quantifiable
2. Tangible and unquantifiable
3. Intangible and quantifiable
4. Intangible and unquantifiable

Answer:

These benefits affect the company's profitability and they are measurable.

These benefits affect the company's profitability but they are difficult to measure.

These benefits do not affect the company's profitability but they are measurable.

These benefits do not affect the company's profitability and they are not measurable.

x

MANAGING STAKEHOLDERS

Managing stakeholders

Stakeholders can be broadly viewed as any group or organization that a business impacts upon or interacts with and can influence the long-term success of that business.

Stakeholders range from small shareholders with a few hundred dollars' worth of shares in a company to communities in which a company has business premises that may employ a few or thousands of people.

Stakeholder knowledge and management is central to the preparation of a comprehensive business case. The balance of critical stakeholders will not be the same in all organizations, but multiple stakeholders must always be taken into account.

The classification of stakeholders is crucial to managing them effectively. They must be classified correctly so that you are aware of the skills and knowledge that they can bring to a project.

Stakeholders can be grouped as

- Customers,

- Employees,
- Suppliers or business partners,
- Community,
- Environment,
- government and regulatory,
- Shareholders and investors.

To be able to manage the stakeholders, it is important to perform an analysis of their positions and the type of power they may be able to exert.

To do this it is necessary to establish a number of issues:

- Who is the key stakeholder?
- Who has the most to lose if the project succeeds?
- Who has the most to gain from the project?
- Whose attitude do you most want to change?
- What capacity does each stakeholder have to help or hinder the project?
- Which stakeholder should you most concentrate your efforts on?

The following steps should be taken to ensure that stakeholders are managed properly:

- identify the relevant stakeholders, pressure groups, and other interested parties,
- assess stakeholder interests in terms of how they will react to the change brought about by the project,
- assess stakeholder commitment or antagonism to the business case,
- assess stakeholder power to promote or hinder the success of the project.

In order to record exactly who the players in your business case are, create a comprehensive map of all the principal stakeholders in the project.

To create a stakeholder map, use the following steps:

- place the name of the project title on a sheet of paper,
- represent each stakeholder individual or group with a circle on the sheet,
- place the most significant stakeholders near the center and other less significant stakeholders around the edge,
- record the way different stakeholders relate to each other using interconnecting lines,
- indicate how relationships between stakeholders may change during the project.

For a business to remain successful in the long term, it must not only deliver against a narrowly focused financial bottom line (concentrating on one stakeholder), but also deliver against a multiple range of stakeholders.

To assess stakeholder interests, record the answers to the following five questions for each stakeholder group:

- What are the priorities, goals, and interests of each group of stakeholders?
- How have they been involved in similar past projects and how might this information be useful with regard to possible reactions during this project?
- What are the possible benefits for each group of stakeholders?
- What are their expectations from the project and what is their attitude to it?
- What is their likely reaction to the investment opportunity and what issues or questions might they raise?

It is essential to assess stakeholder interests in terms of how they will react to the change brought about by the project. This is because if the principal stakeholders are not satisfied, the project will be regarded as a failure. To clarify the position of each stakeholder group, create a table to record each stakeholder's commitment to the project.

To create a commitment assessment table, use the following steps:

- draw a table with seven columns,
- add the following headings to each column - Key stakeholders, Strongly against, Against, Indifferent, Passively in favor, Actively in favor, Strongly in favor,
- record each stakeholder's details in a separate row,
- place an x in the column that best fits the current commitment of a particular stakeholder and a y in the column that corresponds to the level of commitment that is considered adequate,
- use the table to discuss with each group where they are and how they could be encouraged to move to a more positive position.

The position of stakeholders does not remain static and a stakeholder who is in favor of the project, if not handled correctly, may become an opponent. It is for this reason that stakeholder management is critical to the success of a business case.

As well as dividing stakeholders into those who are in favor of the project and those who are against it, it may also be useful to consider stakeholders in terms of how active or passive they are.

To assess how active or passive stakeholders are, create a 2 × 2 matrix with the two dimensions of "Position on the Issue" (whether they are in favor or against it) and "Commitment to Position" (whether they are actively or passively committed).

Fans

The stakeholders in the fans quadrant are actively in favor of the project, have an interest in the results, and are involved in the management of the changes brought about by the project.

Silent partners

The stakeholders in the silent partners quadrant are in favor of the project but play a passive role in the project development and thus have no real influence on the project at all.

Old defenders

The stakeholders in the old defenders quadrant will actively resist the project as they see it as a threat to their current position.

Sleeping dogs

The stakeholders in the sleeping dogs quadrant are not in favor of the project but play a passive role in the project development and thus have no real influence on the project at all.

A stakeholder management program should attempt to:

- position as many of the stakeholders as possible in the fans quadrant,
- minimize the antagonism of stakeholders wherever possible and prevent them from taking a position in the old defenders quadrant,
- move the silent partners up into the top right-hand quadrant where they would become fans,

- move the old defenders down into the bottom left-hand quadrant where they would become sleeping dogs.

Question

Which of the following steps should be taken to ensure that stakeholders are managed properly?

Options:

1. Identify the relevant stakeholders
2. Assess stakeholder power to promote the project
3. Hide planned projects from the stakeholders
4. Assess stakeholder interests
5. Assess stakeholder commitment

Answer:

Option 1: This option is correct. This also involves identifying pressure groups and other interested parties.

Option 2: This option is correct. You should also take into account the stakeholder's power to hinder the success of the project.

Option 3: This option is incorrect. The shareholders should be made aware of upcoming projects, although the information should be presented in a way that is likely to gain a favorable response.

Option 4: This option is correct. You should assess their interests in terms of how they will react to the change brought about by the project.

Option 5: This option is correct. Also, you should try to learn about any possible antagonism to the business case.

By assessing the interests and action of stakeholders, it should be possible to decide how the stakeholders can be influenced to support the project. This assessment will typically involve identifying which project benefits will add value to each group of stakeholders. Stakeholders play an integral role in successful business case development.

Managing the stakeholders of a business case effectively offers a number of benefits. Finding overlooked benefits from those stakeholders who will be using the new product or service will help to overcome resistance to the project.

Developing a new product or service to meet the needs and expectations of a range of stakeholders will gain widespread approval for the project. It is important to remember that the scope of a business case should not be narrowed down to the interests of one group of stakeholders.

Encouraging stakeholders who are not in favor of a new product or service to move to a positive position is an essential step in developing a new project. Minimizing the antagonism of stakeholders wherever possible and preventing them from taking a threatening position will prevent the spread of discontent and opposition to a project.

Effective stakeholder management will prevent unnecessary surprises, which may antagonize stakeholders, during the development stages of the product or service.

Question

Stakeholders play an integral role in successful business case development.

Identify which of the following are possible benefits of effectively managing the stakeholders of a business case.

Options:

1. Finding overlooked benefits from those stakeholders who will be using the new product or service

2. Determining who has most to gain from the development of the product or service

3. Developing the new product or service to meet the needs and expectations of a range of stakeholders

4. Encouraging stakeholders who are not in favor of the product or service to move to a positive position

5. Minimizing the antagonism of stakeholders wherever possible and preventing them from taking a threatening position

6. Preventing unnecessary surprises during the development stages of the product or service

Answer:

Option 1: This option is correct. This will help to overcome resistance to the project.

Option 2: This option is incorrect. The scope of a business case should not be narrowed down to the interests of one group of stakeholders.

Option 3: This option is correct. This will gain widespread approval for the project.

Option 4: This option is correct. This is an essential step in developing a new project.

Option 5: This option is correct. This will prevent the spread of discontent and opposition to the project.

Option 6: This option is correct. Surprises during the development of a project may antagonize stakeholders.

Every important decision during the initiation, planning, and execution stages of a project is made by stakeholders in the organization. As a result, stakeholders can contribute valuable knowledge and skills to the development of a business case. Different stakeholders in an organization make different contributions.

Users and owners

These are the stakeholders who will use and own the new product or service that the project will create. The users and owners detail the needs and specifications necessary to develop the business case.

Sales and marketing staff

Sales and marketing staff promote, price, market, and distribute the idea.

Finance staff

Finance staff coordinate financial data on sales, expenses, and budgets in the organization. Accounting services can analyze the costs and benefits of developing the idea.

IT staff

IT staff can provide information on the technology alternatives or implications of a new product or service.

Legal staff

A company's Legal Department can take care of patent rights and possible liabilities that may arise.

Human Resources staff

The Human Resources Department can allocate the personnel, training, and support necessary to develop the new product or idea.

Research and development staff

The R&D Department can provide staff, time, equipment, and materials necessary to design, test, and modify the idea.

Facilities and equipment staff

The facilities and equipment staff ensure that space, energy, and equipment are available.

Question

Which of these internal stakeholders can contribute valuable information necessary to develop a new product or idea?

Options:

1. Users and owners
2. Marketing staff
3. Legal services staff
4. Human Resources staff
5. Research and development staff 6. Regulatory authorities
7. Finance staff
8. IT staff
9. Facilities and equipment staff

Answer:

Option 1: This option is correct. Users and owners detail the needs and specifications necessary to develop the business case.

Option 2: This option is correct. They are invaluable for promoting, pricing, marketing, and distributing the idea.

Option 3: This option is correct. They can deal with the patent rights and possible liabilities that may arise.

Option 4: This option is correct. They provide the personnel, training, and support necessary to develop the new product or idea.

Option 5: This option is correct. They supply the staff, time, equipment, and materials necessary to design, test, and modify the idea.

Option 6: This option is incorrect. They may be able to supply information about pertinent legislation, but they are not considered an internal stakeholder.

Option 7: This option is correct. They coordinate financial data about the organization, provide accounting services, and can analyze the costs and benefits of developing the idea.

Option 8: This option is correct. They provide information on the technology alternatives or implications of a proposed project.

Option 9: This option is correct. The facilities and equipment staff ensure that the requisite space, energy, and equipment are made available for the project.

George is conducting a meeting with several people who will be working with him on a business case to develop a new information system in a pharmaceutical supplier company.

The new system will integrate sales order entry, inventory management, credit control, production scheduling, and transport scheduling. George has invited the stakeholders to introduce themselves and explain their involvement in the business case. As George conducts the meeting, he invites Lauren to speak first.

Lauren: I'm Lauren from Accounting. As the new information system has minimal financial accounting implications, I'm here to make sure the project stays within budget.

This will involve estimating introduction and continuing costs of implementing the system and figuring out where we can make some savings.

Kenneth: I'm Kenneth from the Sales Department. The idea to implement the new information system came from my department. We are currently using a number of separate mainframe systems and some standalone personal computers.

This system is out of date and leaves us at a competitive disadvantage. We are losing business to competitors who can deliver faster. We need to modernize our systems. Otherwise we will lose 2% to 3% of our turnover per year.

Archie: I'm Archie from the IT Department. I'm going to be working closely with the Sales Department to establish and document the end-user requirements of the new system.

We need to analyze how the existing system works and identify limitations, problems, and opportunities with it. Together we'll need to establish the business objectives that will serve as criteria for the IT team to develop alternative IT solutions.

Mandy: I'm Mandy from the Human Resources Department. If the new information system is introduced, it means better client service and staff reduction in the sales order processing offices.

I'm here to advise on how we should handle relocation of staff and layoffs, if necessary.

In the previous scenario, George listened carefully to how the key stakeholders think they will impact the business case. George analyzes what their contribution to the business case will be.

Lauren

"I'm going to need Lauren's help to obtain financial information about the company, such as the hurdle rate and the rate of return the company requires to fund the project. With Lauren's expertise I'll be able to build a rational cost-benefit picture and also make sure the project stays within the budget."

Kenneth

"Kenneth seems like he will really motivate the team. He's really enthusiastic about implementing the new system and is convinced that it will improve the sales process and increase sales. His vast knowledge of the existing sales system will help determine the needs and specifications of the new information system."

Archie

"Archie's knowledge of business systems and their development is going to be crucial for developing the business case. I'll use Archie's input to write the project scope definition, which clearly defines what the information system will mean for the company and clients."

Mandy

"Mandy will really help with the issue of staff relocation and layoffs. It is estimated that, after the introduction of the new information system, the five sales offices throughout the organization would need 20 to 25 fewer people. The Human Resources Department will estimate the number of these people who will leave the firm due to the normal staff movement, could be used in other departments, or will be laid off. In addition, they will calculate layoff packages and the costs to train those members of staff who would remain in the sales office."

Part of planning a business case involves creating an environment in which Lauren, Kenneth, Archie, and Mandy can contribute their skills and abilities. Feedback and information from these stakeholders will avoid surprises and play an integral role in the development of a successful business case.

Case Study: Question 1 of 4

Scenario

Darren works at Earthfarm, a food manufacturing company. He is writing a business case to develop a specialized organic food supplement for the growing health food market.

Use the Learning Aid The Earthfarm Stakeholders to get the background information on the company and the project.

Darren is now going to talk to members of his team to decide on the scope of the business case. Answer each question to help Darren decide how each stakeholder can assist him with the project.

Question

Darren consults the Research and Development Department. He will require its assistance in a number of areas of the project.

Select the actions where the Research and Development Department can contribute to the project.

Options:

1. Apply food processing and safety procedures for product development
2. Conduct testing
3. Establish the property right of the new supplement
4. Evaluate products against quality standards

Answer:

Option 1: This option is correct. The Research and Development Department will understand the appropriate guidelines.

Option 2: This option is correct. The Research and Development Department supplies the staff, time, equipment, and materials necessary to conduct product testing.

Option 3: This option is incorrect. Establishing property rights for a new product is outside the scope of the Research and Development Department's role.

Option 4: This option is correct. The Research and Development Department will have the expertise in this area and will be aware of the relevant quality standards.

Case Study: Question 2 of 4

Darren consults the Legal Department. Select the area where the Legal Department can contribute to the project.

Options:

1. The Legal Department will not have any contribution to the project
2. Dealing with the procedure and terms required to establish the property rights of the new health food
3. Auditing the cost and benefit analysis of the project

Answer:

Option 1: This option is incorrect. The Legal Department is essential to securing the property rights for the new product.

Option 2: This option is correct. The Legal Department will deal with patent rights and possible liabilities that may arise

Option 3: This option is incorrect. This type of financial analysis is outside the scope of the Legal Department.

Case Study: Question 3 of 4

Darren knows that the Marketing Department can contribute to the project in a number of areas.

Select the ways in which Marketing can help the project.

Options:

1. Researching concepts, texture issues, appropriate sweetness, flavors, and aromas

2. Conducting taste panel testing and getting feedback from clients

3. Conducting interviews for research and development vacancies

Answer:

Option 1: This option is correct. The Marketing Department is responsible for carrying out research into consumer preferences.

Option 2: This option is correct. The Marketing Department will liaise with the clients and customers in order to get their views on the new product.

Option 3: This option is incorrect. This is not the responsibility of the Marketing Department. Marketing is responsible for promoting, pricing, marketing, and distributing the idea.

Case Study: Question 4 of 4

How will Darren utilize the Human Resources Department?

What contributions will it make to the project?

Options:

1. Supplying information on how to obtain patents

2. Supplying specifications for new personnel and training that may be required to develop the new health food

3. Supplying the details on available existing personnel

Answer:

Option 1: This option is incorrect. This is not the responsibility of the Human Resources Department.

Option 2: This option is correct. The Human Resources Department has the expertise required to draw up the specifications for the new staff that the company will need for the project.

Option 3: This option is correct. The Human Resources Department will have access to information about all the staff in the company.

In this topic you have learned the benefits of correctly identifying the stakeholders for a project of a business case, and the methods you should use to manage the project stakeholders.

IDENTIFYING THE DECISION MAKERS

Identifying the decision makers

To develop a successful business case, you must accurately determine who the decision makers are and the criteria they will use to make the investment decision. Who approves the business case depends on how the company is organized, as well as the size and scope of its activities.

If your company is very large, decisions for new products and services may lie with a division president, rather than with the CEO or chairman of the board. If your company is very small, perhaps only the owners or partners are the decision makers. Sometimes one person makes the decision, while in other circumstances the decision may lie on the opinions of a group of people.

As you prepare your case, you need to determine the groups that will decide the feasibility of your project and document their details by name, responsibility, and decision-process role. Make sure the highest-level decision maker is accurately identified.

Some suggested groups of people who may be the decision makers within your company include:

- company owners and executives,
- corporate directors,
- stockholders,
- research and development representatives,
- sales and marketing representatives,
- financial services and accounting representatives.

To make a decision to commit to a project, company owners and executives will want to satisfy themselves that the following questions about the product or service have been properly answered:

- How does the new product or service relate to the present business?
- What business value will the product or service achieve?
- How much will it cost to develop and market the new product or service?
- How will this cost affect company profits?
- How does the new product or service relate to our corporate strategy?

Corporate directors and stockholders will want to know the following:

- How is stock going to be affected by introducing the new product or service?
- What will be the cost of the new product or service?
- How will the cost affect stock dividends?
- Are the financial projections healthy and realistic?
- How much will it cost to develop and market the new product or service?

- What are the financial risks associated with developing the product or service?

Sales and marketing may be interested in whether the project will satisfy consumer needs profitably:

- Is there a market for this product or service?
- Is the market ready for this product?
- What similar products or services are being offered by competitors?
- How will we price the product?
- What retailers would carry the product?
- How would we promote the product?

Finally, the Research and Development Department will ask the following questions:

- Do we have the expertise to produce the product or service?
- Will we need to modify this product for production?
- What would it cost to modify?
- Are there any possible production problems?
- Where will we get supplies and raw materials?
- How reliable and secure are these supplies?

Decision criteria are factors (both tangible and intangible) used by decision makers to determine the attractiveness of investment alternatives.

A CEO concerned with enterprise strategy and operations may be interested in different benefits than an accounting communications manager responsible for reducing the costs of phone services.

There are a number of common pitfalls in identifying criteria:

- asking the right people, who give wrong answers (either inadvertently or on purpose),

- getting the right answers from the right people, but then having the business case team inadvertently misinterpret such remarks,
- being unable to contact the right people because they are unavailable or have not been identified,
- overlooking valuable secondary sources, such as publications.

In order to be confident that the business case you propose addresses the key decision criteria, you should work through the following steps:

- identify at least one criterion for each decision maker,
- link the value of your product or service to personal concerns of individual decision makers,
- express criteria in language understood by each level of decision maker,
- express each criterion in terms of a benefit to be realized,
- weigh all criteria to indicate their relative importance to the decision.

One way to find out details about the decision criteria is to conduct a brainstorming session with all decision makers or their representatives.

During these sessions, you can find out about any concerns decision makers may have, but also about any other goals or opportunities that may arise in the future.

Other recommended ways of finding out details about your decision criteria include:

- reviewing publications from vendors, consultants, and other groups knowledgeable in the area being evaluated by the business case,

- asking expert acquaintances in the subject matter of the content of the business case talking to "organizational neighbors",
- searching through business articles profiling similar cost-benefit analysis.

Correctly identifying the decision makers allows you to: identify factors

Correctly identifying the decision makers for a business case helps to identify the factors that will influence the decision makers with regards to a business case.

discover criteria

When you know who the decision makers are, you can then go on to discover the criteria that are important to them when considering a business case.

focus resources

Correct identification of decision makers helps to focus the team's resources on areas that are important to the final investment decision, increasing the business case's chance of success.

gather information

It helps to understand the information requirements of the different decision makers, allowing you to gather the information suited to their needs.

Question

Identify the benefits of correctly identifying the decision makers of a business case.

Options:

1. It helps to identify the factors that will influence the decision makers with regards to a business case.
2. It helps when selecting the team required to produce the business case

3. It helps to focus the team's resources on areas that are important to the final investment decision

4. It helps when developing the information requirements of the different decision makers

Answer:

Option 1: This option is correct. When you know who the decision makers are, you can then go on to discover the criteria that are important to them when considering a business case.

Option 2: This option is incorrect. The decision makers do not produce the business case.

Option 3: This option is correct. Your team can concentrate on the areas that are important to the decision makers, increasing the business case's chance of success.

Option 4: This option is correct. Identifying the decision makers allows you to gather the information suited to their needs.

CONVINCING DECISION MAKERS

Convincing decision makers

The way in which you present your business case will really influence how your audience will react to your case.

If you are well prepared, with information and numbers to support your arguments, you will be more likely to present your idea with confidence and persuade the decision makers about the feasibility of your project.

To convince the decision makers about the feasibility of your project, do the following:

- be sure of your information,
- use credible sources to support your arguments,
- deliver your message with a clear strategy,
- use numbers, graphs, and charts to support your arguments.

The best preparation to argue your case successfully is to be sure of the information you present.

If you have done your research well, you will be able to produce facts and figures for which there is no debate. To add strength to your arguments, make sure you use credible sources - ones that are respected in your industry.

People can only process so much information at one time. You should choose the most suitable strategy to fit the decision makers' style of listening and the message you are trying to deliver to them. A basic rule of thumb is to give the general idea first and then back it up with facts.

The problem with using the reverse approach (giving the facts first and then following with your conclusion) is that the decision makers may understand the facts and reach an entirely different conclusion. When you are sure of your facts, you should choose a strategy with a persuasive style that brings home the main ideas you want to present to your decision makers.

First, write out all the main ideas that you want to present. To ensure that you do not lose people along the way, keep in mind these guidelines:

- keep your examples and information as simple and timely as possible,
- choose images that are familiar to your audience to support your ideas,
- keep in mind the perspective of the decision makers.

You can use a number of strategies to develop your logic and arguments for your business case. These strategies include:

chronological

It is very helpful in walking the listeners through a series of events in the order they occurred. It can also assist listeners in connecting events where you may wish to show a cause-and-effect relationship between the events. Finally, this strategy is helpful in situations where the audience needs to look at the past, present, and future.

topical

A topical strategy involves presenting a variety of topics. This is a very popular approach in technical areas, but it is not very persuasive in its orientation. If you use this strategy, be very careful to establish the relationship between the topics. This transition between topics is critical to success.

problem/solution

A problem/solution strategy cycles back and forth between stating a problem and then solving that problem. If your audience analysis suggests that the audience will have a variety of questions about your topic, this is a good approach. It will allow you to anticipate the questions and provide the answers. A variation of this strategy is the question/answer, in which you pose the questions and then answer them for the listener.

most critical to least critical

The most critical to least critical strategy is very useful where a series of variables have had an impact on the outcome of the proposed solution. Start with the most critical elements and move to those that are less critical or more common. For example, if you were considering outsourcing work for a project, some qualities would be very critical in presenting the company you outsource to. You would want to highlight those critical factors first and then move progressively to those qualities that all the companies possessed.

In terms of delivering your message to decision makers, you may need to use more than one delivery strategy. Typical delivery approaches include:

big picture/small picture

The aim of this approach is to tie your ideas or solutions to the overall goals of the company, department, or client. You explain how your ideas will help the listeners achieve these goals. This approach helps the decision makers to see how your project aligns with the larger goals of the department, division, or company.

procedural

The procedural approach lays out a procedure in a step-by-step fashion. If there are a number of steps to the procedure, there is a danger that people will begin to tune out. The best way around that is to break multiple steps into two, three, or four groups or categories.

compare/contrast

The compare/contrast approach advocates comparing and contrasting. For example, you might use this strategy to demonstrate how you are different from the competition. This strategy allows you to stress the differentiation that is important to the decision makers.

motivated sequence

Using the motivated sequence approach, you establish with the decision makers that you have identified a problem or opportunity that is of concern to them, explain how your project can address the issue, and, then ask the decision makers to provide the resources you need to make the project a reality. This strategy is used to sell a business case to the decision makers.

spatial

With the spatial strategy, you are trying to get the audience members to literally see something "in their mind's eye." For example, if you wanted to describe what you saw on a trip abroad, you might use the spatial strategy to allow the audience to travel with you in their minds and "see" what you saw.

Question

You can use a number of strategies when presenting a business case.

Match each delivery strategy with its description. Drag the letters on the left to the boxes on the right. Use each letter only once.

Options:

A. Big picture/small picture

B. Compare/contrast

C. Spatial

D. Motivated sequence

Targets:

1. Describe how your project is different from other projects

2. Identify an issue that is of concern to the decision makers, explain how your project addresses the issue, and ask the decision makers to provide the resources required for the project

3. Show how the project goals tie in with the larger goals of the department or company

4. Get the decision makers to visualize the project and the benefits it will bring

Answer:

This is a description of the compare/contrast approach. This strategy allows you to stress the differences between proposed projects that are important to the decision makers.

This is a description of the motivated sequence approach. This strategy is used to sell a proposed project to the decision makers in an organization.

This is a description of the big picture/small picture approach. The aim of this approach is to tie your ideas or solutions to the overall goals of the company, department, or client.

This is a description of the spatial strategy. With the spatial strategy, you are trying to get the audience members to see the benefits your project can offer.

No matter how well you have conducted your research and presented your business case to suit the particular audience, the chances are that there will always be someone within your company who will have doubts about your idea.

One technique that can help persuade the decision makers about the feasibility of your business case is to use numbers.

You can use numbers in the following ways to persuade the decision makers:

- for impact,
- to show projections - if possible, the projections should be for three to five years in the future,
- to show historical performance data about similar products: this information should go back five years if possible,
- to show how your product will be better than similar products,
- to forecast industry trends.

Numbers, whether they are in text or graphics, are highly persuasive and arguing against them is very difficult. Numbers can show history and project the future.

Question

Select the methods you should use to convince the decision makers about the feasibility of your project.

Options:

1. Be sure of your information
2. Use credible sources to support your arguments
3. Deliver your message with a clear strategy
4. Use numbers, graphs, and charts to support your arguments
5. Use the same level of analysis that is applied to every aspect of the business case

Answer:

Option 1: This option is correct. If you have done your research well, you will be able to produce facts and figures for which there is no argument.

Option 2: This option is correct. Make sure you use credible sources, ones that are respected in your industry.

Option 3: This option is correct. People can only process so much information at one time: choose the most suitable strategy to fit the decision makers' style of listening and the message you are trying to deliver to them.

Option 4: This option is correct. Numbers, whether they are in text or graphics, are highly persuasive and arguing against them is very difficult.

Option 5: This option is incorrect. The level of analysis for a particular aspect of a case should be tailored to the audience.

SECTION 3 - SECTIONS OF A BUSINESS CASE

SECTION 3 - Sections of a Business Case

There are a number of benefits to dividing a business case into sections. Decision makers are more likely to view the business case document positively if it is easy to use and understand. Information presented in manageable chunks is more likely to maintain the interest of an audience. Also, the significance of each section will be readily apparent. This topic will examine the purpose and contents of each section of a business case.

In this topic, you have learned about the information that should be contained in the start of a business case document, and how important it is as a part of an effective business case proposal. In this topic, you have learned about the information that should be contained in the main body of a business case document.

DIVIDING A BUSINESS CASE INTO CLEARLY IDENTIFIABLE SECTIONS

Dividing a business case into clearly identifiable sections

The business case document is the primary output from the business case preparation and provides the project team with a roadmap to guide project execution through good and bad times.

The business case functions as a:

message sender

The business case document as a message sender communicates your team's ideas and message to many different audiences. It enables everyone affected by the project (employees, directors, lenders, and potential investors) to be knowledgeable about the project.

motivational tool

The business case document can work as a motivational tool by communicating the project team's vision of your project. Without this, it would be impossible to motivate people when they do not know where they are going or what they are trying to achieve.

management development tool

The business case document is a management development tool because it forces the team to think about problems, competitive conditions, and situations that are or may be beneficial or harmful to the project.

performance measurement tool

The business case document acts as a performance tool because it states the goals and objectives for a project. If approved, it will also provide a basis for evaluating the project performance in the future.

The quality of the business case document is crucial to win the attention of the decision makers. The business case document must have the right content, be organized into logical and clearly defined sections, and be presented in a way that is informative and maintains the audience's interest.

Decision makers are more likely to view the business case document positively if it is easy to use and understand. Also, the significance of each section will be clearer to the reader. This lesson examines the contents of a business case document. After you have taken this lesson, you will be able to identify the elements in the main body of a formal proposal.

Question

There are benefits to splitting a business case into sections. What are they?

Options:

1. Decision makers are more likely to view the business case document positively if it is easy to use and understand
2. The significance of each section will be clearer to the reader

3. Information presented in manageable chunks is more likely to maintain the audience's interest

4. It reduces the amount of information that the case must contain

Answer:

Option 1: This option is correct. Dividing the information into sections makes it easier to understand and increases the chances that people will read the document.

Option 2: This option is correct. Organizing your information and placing it in sections will help the audience to understand the significance of a piece of information, and will allow them to place it in the context of the overall project.

Option 3: This option is correct. When the information is presented in manageable pieces the reader is less likely to feel overwhelmed by the amount of material that they need to read.

Option 4: This option is incorrect. Dividing a business case into sections does not reduce the amount of information that it should contain, however, it does make information easier to find.

APPROPRIATE PROJECT TITLES

Appropriate project titles

There are many ways to organize and present the introduction or opening of a business case document. In general, a business case should include the following components:

title page

The title page contains the title of the business case.

table of contents

The table of contents makes the business case document easy to use and understand.

executive summary

The executive summary reports on organizational issues and outcomes of the business case.

mission statement

The mission statement concisely describes the aim of the project.

objectives

The objectives describe clearly and precisely what the project is expected to deliver.

purpose of the business case

The purpose describes the problem or opportunity that the project will address.

situational assessment and problem statement

The situational assessment and problem statement establishes the benefit to the organization for proceeding with the project.

Decision makers are more likely to view the business case document positively if it is easy to use and understand.

A table of contents is an important organizer for the entire document and makes it easier to find information within. Some readers may not be interested in everything and will want to locate specific information quickly.

The table of contents lists the major headings in the business case and the page on which each is found.

Question

Match each component of the introduction to a business case document with its purpose by dragging the letter associated with each component to the description of its purpose. Use each letter only once.

Options:

A. Situational assessment and problem statement

B. Table of contents

C. Objectives

D. Mission statement

E. Critical assumptions and constraints

F. Executive summary

Targets:

1. Describes concisely what the aim of the project is

2. Reports on organizational issues and outcomes of the business case

3. Makes the business case document easy to use and understand

4. Describes clearly and precisely what the project is expected to deliver

5. Establishes the benefit to the organization for proceeding with the project

6. Records critical assumptions and constraints made during the planning process

Answer:

This describes the role of the mission statement. It informs the audience of the intent of the business case.

This describes the role of the executive summary. It reports on organizational issues and outcomes of the business case.

This describes the role of the table of contents. It is an organizer for the entire document and makes it easier to find information. It lists the major headings in the business case and the page on which each is found.

This describes the purpose of the objectives. They describe what the project is expected to deliver.

This describes the function of the situational assessment and problem statement. It establishes the benefit to the organization for proceeding with the project.

This describes the role of the critical assumptions and constraints section of the business case.

The title page is the first impression a reader gets of a business case. It should be neat and orderly, simple, balanced, and easy to read.

It should contain the:

- title of the project,
- project designation,
- name of the organization,

- date of approval by the organization.

You get better results if you create a substantive project title that states a benefit to the organization, for example: "Improving Customer Retention by Improved Database Performance" or "Improving Conditions and Benefits to Reduce Staff Turnover."

You should try to construct a project title that does the following:

- describes the recommendation in terms of its outcome or impact on the organization,
- contains a verb that expresses a beneficial state of change for the organization,
- focuses on results and not product or service names,
- avoids any use of in-house jargon and generic titles.

Question

What should your project title do?

Options:

1. Describe the recommendation in terms of its outcome
2. Contain a verb that expresses a beneficial state of change for the organization
3. Describe the assumptions and constraints that underpin the project
4. Focus on results
5. Avoid any use of in-house jargon and generic titles

Answer:

Option 1: This option is correct. The title should focus on the project's outcome or impact on the organization.

Option 2: This option is correct. The title should succinctly describe the change that the project will bring about in the organization.

Option 3: This option is incorrect. The assumptions and constraints should be outlined in the main body of the business case document.

Option 4: This option is correct. The title must focus on results rather than product or service names.

Option 5: This option is correct. The title must clearly express improvements and benefits to the organization that the project will bring.

Stuart is an executive for Trafficka, a successful fashion franchise. He has stated that if a business case title is flawed, he will not read the case itself.

Here is a list of project titles for business cases that Stuart has examined recently:

Improving Productivity through Improved Data-sharing Technology - This title is acceptable because it focuses on results.

Reducing Manufacturing Times through Automated Quality Program - This title contains a verb that describes a beneficial state to the organization and focuses on results.

A Suggestion for Trafficka - This business case was rejected because the title is too vague.

Analyzing ZipFasten Model 200 - This business case was rejected because the title relies on in-house jargon rather than addressing specific benefits to the company.

Proposal to Assess Document Review Procedures - This business case was rejected. The title does not express a beneficial result for the organization.

Question

Identify which of the following examples are appropriate project titles for a business case.

Options:

1. Improving Productivity through Online Inventory Access
2. Proposal to Assess Internet Security Requirements
3. Increasing Customer Satisfaction through Improved Service Options
4. A Proposal for New American Corporation
5. Reducing Time in the Manufacturing Process through Automated Quality Program
6. Analyzing TurboTremor Model 1200

Answer:

Option 1: This option is correct. This title focuses on results.

Option 2: This option is incorrect. This title does not express a beneficial result for the organization.

Option 3: This option is correct. It focuses on results and the benefit to the organization.

Option 4: This option is incorrect. This title is too vague.

Option 5: This option is correct. This title contains a verb that describes a beneficial state to the organization and focuses on results.

Option 6: This option is incorrect. This title relies on in-house jargon.

x

THE EXECUTIVE SUMMARY

The executive summary

The executive summary is the single most important part of the business case document.

It is the part of the document that most people will read first, if not the only part, and it's the only part

that's likely to be read by all decision makers.

The executive summary should focus on

- why the project is necessary and why it is the best solution,
- the most important reasons for recommending the project,
- the most important benefits of the project to the organization,
- the costs of the project and major disadvantages, if any,
- how the project relates to the corporate strategy.

The executive summary reports on organizational issues and outcomes of the business case rather than the reasoning behind it.

There is no need to include assumptions and constraints (unless they are key), background (except for perhaps one sentence), analysis, or technical descriptions. The executive summary should have a concise length and summary format to enable the reader to quickly understand the project plans.

When writing the executive summary, keep these guidelines in mind:

- write the executive summary so that it is accessible to anyone from the janitor to the chairman of the board,
- organize the information in the executive summary into bulleted or numbered points for ease of reading,
- keep the executive summary short – 1 to 2 pages for the first 25 pages of the business case document,
- and an additional page for each 50 pages thereafter,
- develop the executive summary after the rest of the document has been completed.

Question

Mark works in the Sales Department of a company that sells digital products and services. He is writing a business case to look for funding to install a new voice messaging system in the company. Identify the information that Mark should include in the executive summary.

Options:

1. Newark Message Network will reduce overall costs and increase customer satisfaction and revenue opportunities.

2. Sales analysis reveals that 50 calls drop off the sales line every day. This amounts to lost revenue from sales of $1.5 million per annum.

3. Newark Message Network will develop corporate strategy by improving the image of the organization.

4. A total of 40% of 800 polled customers stated that they were satisfied with the after-sale service at the company.

5. All payoff area calculations reflect 75% of full-year benefits for Year 1 of this analysis, rather than 100%.

Answer:

Option 1: This option is correct. This is a benefit to the organization and should be included in the summary.

Option 2: This option is incorrect. The summary should not contain background information and analysis.

Option 3: This option is correct. This shows how the project relates to corporate strategy and should be included in the summary.

Option 4: This option is incorrect. The summary should not contain analysis.

Option 5: This option is incorrect. This information contains analysis, which should be dealt with in the

main body of the business case rather than in the executive summary.

MISSION STATEMENTS

Mission statements

The mission statement is a concise, general, high-level description of what the project is expected to deliver. It explains what is to be done, for whom, and why. If possible, it should not exceed one sentence.

A mission statement should say who your company is, what you do, why you do it, and what you stand for. The contents of a mission statement will vary from company to company.

You may find it useful to examine other companies' mission statements. For example: "Brocadero offers a complete editorial, electronic pagination, and archiving system designed specially for newspapers and magazines."

Ensure your statement is about you and not some other company. You should not copy a statement.

Question

You have been asked to choose a mission statement for Lena Lang.

Lena Lang is a successful high-street fashion brand for men and women. Every season, a new collection is designed and created and then sold exclusively at Lena Lang stores throughout the world. Orders are delivered to outlets twice weekly.

Select the most appropriate mission statement for the company.

Options:

1. Lena Lang is a fashion and design house.

2. Lena Lang responds to customer tastes and concerns to respond rapidly to market demands for clothes and fashion items.

3. Lena Lang is a successful high-street fashion brand. It has achieved this position through a combination of creative fashion design and a rapid response to market demands. The concerns and tastes of customers are channeled from individual stores to the company's design team.

4. Lena Lang listens to the concerns and tastes of customers. They are channeled from individual stores to the company's design team. Lena Lang has a number of stores.

Answer:

Option 1: This option is incorrect. This mission statement gives insufficient information.

Option 2: This option is correct. It precisely and concisely describes the company's method of operation.

Option 3: This option is incorrect. It describes the company, but does not describe its business practices.

Option 4: This option is incorrect. This mission statement is too long and it is too vague. It does not focus on results.

OBJECTIVES TO BE INCLUDED IN THE BUSINESS CASE

Objectives to be included in the business case

The objectives of the business case should clearly and precisely describe what the project is expected to deliver.

They include such items as:

- products, services, or technologies to be developed or utilized,
- problems or issues resolved,
- barriers to growth that will be overcome,
- increased volume of domestic or export sales,
- new partnerships or linkages created.

Each objective should be Specific, Measurable, Achievable, Realistic, and Timely (SMART). It should be clear how each objective relates to predefined organizational goals and corporate strategy.

Such hard data verifies the value of the project and makes it an attractive investment to the decision makers. For example, you could give data on the increase in turnover that will result from the installation of a new order processing system.

Objectives must communicate information about the project simply and clearly. A manager examines a document that lists a number of proposed objectives for a project to develop a traffic bypass. Some were used, but others were rejected as unsuitable:

the new bypass will create an annual savings of $300,000 in maintenance on other roads - This is unsuitable. It is not relevant to the project and should not be included.

the new bypass will reduce travel time required to reach the main highway by five minutes - This objective is usable - it describes an issue that will be resolved.

the new bypass will reduce traffic flow using other routes by 25% - This is a benefit that is not directly related to the project, so it should not be listed as an objective.

the new bypass will attract new industry that will provide 150 new jobs - This objective is measurable and should be included.

Question

Darren works for Earthfarm. He is writing a business case to seek funding for a new project. Which of the following examples are valid objectives for the project?

Options:

1. The new supplement will reduce the number of customers who are ordering a similar supplement from competing firms
2. The new supplement will increase turnover by $2 million

3. The increased profits that the company will earn from the supplement can be invested in the Research and Development Department

4. Developing the supplement may increase staff morale in a number of areas

Answer:

Option 1: This option is correct. This describes an issue that will be resolved.

Option 2: This option is correct. This objective is measurable.

Option 3: This option is incorrect. This is not relevant to the project and should not be included.

Option 4: This option is incorrect. This is a benefit that is not directly related to the project, and, as such, it should not be included in the objectives.

THE MAIN BODY OF THE FORMAL PROPOSAL

The main body of the formal proposal

A business case document consists of an opening section followed by the main body of the proposal. The main body of the proposal describes the solution of the project. It provides the information that enables key decision makers to decide whether the project should be undertaken at all.

The main body of the formal proposal is the crux of your business case proposal. The main body of a business case proposal may include the:

needs assessment

The needs assessment contains the situational assessment or the problem statement. This should clearly establish the situation that currently exists that will be exploited or solved by the project. It should contain a description of the relevant environmental conditions, an assessment of how the business needs are currently being met, or not met, or an analysis of the gap between the current situation and the stated objectives.

technical analysis

The technical analysis provides a more detailed technical analysis of the implications of the situational assessment and problem statement.

project work plan

This covers the implementation strategy, which is the plan that covers how the solution to the problem or opportunity will be put into action.

financial plan

This gives the details of the Benefit/Cost/Risk Analysis.

project team

This contains a list of the people who will be responsible for implementing the project, and contains relevant information about the team members.

appendix

This section of the business case contains all references, case studies, and testimonials that are referred to in the main body of the business case.

Each element in the main body should have a section introduction.

You should format this paragraph appropriately to highlight it. Consider the use of a larger font size, bolding, shading, and so on.

This focuses the reader's attention and helps the reader to make the transition from one major concept to the next, and gives you an opportunity to state your key themes.

When writing the elements in the main body of the business case, you should

- stay focused on the controlling strategy you established in the executive summary,
- be objective,

- use specific, concrete language,
- support your claims with substantive evidence.

Question

Which elements should be included in the main body of a business case?

Options:

1. Needs assessment
2. Technical analysis
3. Table of contents
4. Financial plan
5. Project work plan
6. Project team
7. Appendix

Answer:

Option 1: This option is correct. The needs assessment contains the situational assessment or the problem statement.

Option 2: This option is correct. This provides a more detailed technical analysis of the implications of the situational assessment and problem statement

Option 3: This option is incorrect. This is not required in the main body of the proposal.

Option 4: This option is correct. This gives the details of the Benefit/Cost/Risk Analysis.

Option 5: This option is correct. This covers the implementation strategy for the project.

Option 6: This option is correct. This contains a list of the people who will be responsible for implementing the project.

Option 7: This option is correct. This can contain references, case studies, and testimonials.

The project work plan covers the implementation strategy, which is the plan that covers how the solution to the problem or opportunity will be put into action.

The project work plan should include:

key activities and locations

A project consists of a number of activities in a specific location. Examples include setting up a new database system, or updating a company's network.

milestones and timelines for completion

A project must deliver measurable results within a predetermined time frame. If you are seeking funding for a project, you must be able to give estimates of when it will generate results. For example, you could say that a new order processing system will be active in three months, and will double the company's processing ability in six months.

the time frame for beginning and completing each task in the project

The plan must contain a breakdown of the time required for each task in the project. For example, in the case of a project to relocate an office, the overall project may be broken down into smaller tasks such as securing a new premises, moving furniture, installing a network, and so on.

the risks

The plan must document the risks associated with the project. For example, if a project is unsuccessful, the company may lose money, or it may lose out on pursuing other opportunities.

the project staff

The plan must list the staff members who will work on the project. This may be a small group of people in some projects, or it could be entire departments, or the project could be outsourced.

Question

What should be included in the project work plan?

Options:

1. Key activities and locations
2. Assumptions and constraints
3. Time frame for beginning and completing each task in the project
4. Milestones and timelines for completion
5. Project staff
6. Risks

Answer:

Option 1: This option is correct. The plan must include a list of the activities that the project will require. The plan must state where these activities will be carried out.

Option 2: This option is incorrect. The plan must state how the plan will be carried out. It does not require the assumptions and constraints that were factors in deciding on the plan.

Option 3: This option is correct. The plan should contain a detailed schedule for each task in the project.

Option 4: This option is correct. The plan should forecast the completion of different phases of the project.

Option 5: This option is correct. The plan should contain information about the staff members who will implement the project.

Option 6: This option is correct. The plan should make the audience aware of any risks associated with the project.

The financial plan in a business case gives the details of the Benefit/Cost/Risk Analysis. A financial plan should include information in a number of categories:

detailed budget

The financial plan must contain a detailed budget that gives a breakdown of all the costs associated with the project.

pricing

The plan must list the prices of the items that must be purchased in order to carry out the project.

cost analysis

The plan should give a detailed analysis of all costs incurred by the project.

sources of funding

All the sources of funding for the project should be given.

returns from project performance (with time)

The plan should give the project returns from the project according to a specified time frame. This will help the audience to evaluate the benefits of the project.

operating and administrative costs

If the project is going to bring about a change in work practices, the operating and administrative costs associated with the new procedures must be listed.

The business case should give information about the project team, the people who will be responsible for implementing the project. It should contain details on the following:

project team

All the people who will work on the project must be listed.

resumes

The resume of each member of the team must be available for inspection by the business case audience.

org chart

The org chart displays the team hierarchy and shows how the team is structured.

subcontractors

All subcontractors that elements of the project may be outsourced to must be listed.

partner profile

The business case must contain a profile of any industry partners that may be involved in the project.

CHAPTER 2 - WRITING A BUSINESS CASE

CHAPTER 2 - Writing a Business Case

SECTION 1 - INTRODUCTION TO BUSINESS CASES

SECTION 1 - Introduction to Business Cases

Every business wants good solutions for the issues and opportunities facing it. But sometimes the best solutions are bypassed due to a lack of coherent information. Documenting all the relevant information in a business case makes it easier to link the issues to the solution, and encourages the decision makers in your organization to invest in your project.

In this lesson, you will find out more about the benefits of writing a good business case for a proposed project, and obtain an overview of the key issues that an effective business case should address.

A business case defines a problem or opportunity, and outlines the steps that you intend to take to deal with the issue or opportunity. It can also serve as a project blueprint to be referred to throughout the project's life cycle. The main function of a business case is to describe the problem or opportunity facing the company, what will happen if the project is not implemented, how the project will address the issue, how the project will be implemented, and the resources required to implement the project.

It can help the decision maker to compare proposed projects, clarify complex information, and make an objective decision.

A business case defines your project and its goals. It also helps you to allocate resources, make provisions for unforeseen obstacles, and facilitate good decision making. A business case should answer important questions about your proposed project.

A good business case should contain a background; an executive summary; a situational assessment and problem statement; a project description; a solution description; a cost and benefit analysis; an implementation timeline; a critical assumptions and risk assessment section; and a conclusions and recommendations section.

The marketing components section of your business case includes information on how to reach customers and create sales.

The five marketing components that should be included in a business case are the research plan, the product features and benefits, the creative plan, the marketing communications plan, and the sales plan. The marketing components of a business case are often interlinked and interdependent.

WRITING A GOOD BUSINESS CASE

Writing a good business case

Being aware of the benefits of creating a good business case can help to motivate you and your team.

It is important that you know when it is appropriate to write a business case, and that you have a clear vision of what you hope to achieve with it. A business case is, above all, a selling tool. You use a business case to persuade senior executives in your organization that your proposed project is more deserving of budget approval than other competing bids.

A well-written business case benefits you and your organization by allowing you to:

gain control of resources

A good business case can help you gain control of resources by convincing executives to choose your project as the best available response to a problem or opportunity.

calculate the potential benefits of the project

The business case serves as a yardstick for a project, allowing you to measure its success. It can also facilitate benefit evaluation by outlining the "do nothing" scenario -

that is, what will happen to the business if the project is not undertaken. This effectively links the issues to the solution.

simplify the development of the financial justification

A good business case simplifies the development of the financial justification, and can identify holes or problems with the solution. However, a business case should be more than just a financial document.

provide a consistent message to many audiences

A good business case provides a high-level and consistent view of the entire project to all parties potentially affected by the project.

share and organize thoughts, activities, and knowledge

A business case provides an objective review of the ideas and facts of the project, identifies inconsistencies or weaknesses, and communicates the purpose of the project. It also justifies your team's effort, and gives your team a sense of accomplishment.

Jan's business case gives the decision makers in her company a comprehensive overview of her project's potential.

By outlining the "do nothing" scenario, the business case helps to emphasize the problems in the existing payroll system and clarify how Jan's solution will address these issues.

The business case gives the decision makers all the information they need to weigh the pros and cons of Jan's proposed project.

Question

How can writing a good business case benefit you and your organization?

Options:

1. By helping you to gain control of resources
2. By enabling you to disguise project inconsistencies or weaknesses
3. By replacing a financial document
4. By facilitating the calculation of the potential benefits of a project
5. By delivering a consistent message to different audiences
6. By enabling your team to share and organize thoughts, activities, and knowledge

Answer:

Option 1: This is a correct option. A good business case can persuade executives to choose your project as the best available response to a problem or opportunity.

Option 2: This is an incorrect option. A good business case identifies any inconsistencies or weaknesses in a proposed project.

Option 3: This is an incorrect option. Although it does facilitate the development of a financial justification for the project, a business case is not just a financial document.

Option 4: This is a correct option. The business case provides a useful measurement of the project's success. It can also outline what will happen to the business if the project is not undertaken.

Option 5: This is a correct option. A good business case provides a high-level and consistent view of the entire project to all parties potentially affected by the project.

Option 6: This is a correct option. A business case reviews and organizes the ideas and facts of the project, identifies inconsistencies or weaknesses, and communicates the purpose of the project.

x

FUNCTIONS OF A BUSINESS CASE

Functions of a business case

A business case gives key decision makers an overview of a project. It can also help you to secure the resources you require for a project. When writing a business case, you should bear in mind its function - what you and the decision maker want the business case to do.

A business case defines a problem or opportunity, and outlines the steps that you intend to take to deal with the problem or opportunity. You use a business case to convince the decision makers in your organization that your project is deserving of resources.

A business case also serves as a project blueprint, which can be referred to throughout the project life cycle to ensure that everything stays on track. The main functions of a business case are to describe:

- the problem or opportunity facing the company,
- what will happen if the project is not implemented,
- how the project will address the issue,
- how the project will be implemented,

- the resources required to implement the project.

Sam is a regional manager for a clothing retail company. Having identified a fall in sales revenue in some outlets on the West coast, he proposes to consolidate some of these outlets to reduce costs. In his business case, he gives details of the downturn in sales in these outlets. He provides a "do nothing" scenario, stating that inaction on this issue will result in increased costs and possible damage to the company's brand image.

Sam's business case proposes to address the issue by consolidating several West-coast retail outlets into two bigger outlets in prestige locations. It describes how each phase of the consolidation will be executed, and provides an estimate of the personnel and financial resources that will be needed to implement the project.

The information in a well-written business case can enable the decision maker to do a number of things.

Compare proposed projects

The decision maker needs to compare the recommendations, pricing, and evidence in your business case with those for other proposed projects. She may have to deal with a lot of conflicting information, and may have little practical knowledge of the subject area.

Clarify complex information

A business case can enable a non-technical decision maker to understand crucial technical information relating to the proposed project.

Make an objective decision

A business case adds objectivity to the decision-making process by providing specific, organized, and detailed information about the proposed project.

Amanda is a senior executive in a software company. She has received two business cases from two IT managers, each proposing a solution for upgrading the corporate intranet.

She needs to compare a lot of information in order to make an informed decision regarding which project to approve. Because Amanda is not very familiar with the technical aspects of this area, she needs the business cases to explain crucial technical information concisely and without jargon.

Amanda also wants her decision to be objective and based solely on the information provided in the business cases. Information in a business case should be presented to executives like Amanda in a way that facilitates decision making. All potential benefits of the project should be summarized in clear business terms. This makes it easier for decision makers like Amanda to evaluate the business case.

Question

You are presenting a business case to your company, a clothing manufacturer, for the outsourcing of particular manufactured components of your clothing products. What are the functions of your business case in this scenario?

Options:

1. To outline the increased revenue to be made from outsourcing expensive manufacturing elements
2. To describe how the company will lose market share to rivals with cheaper products unless it outsources
3. To provide technical information about the software requirements of the project

4. To propose a detailed outsourcing plan to enable the company to retain its market share

5. To outline the schedule for implementation of the plan

6. To provide investors with data on projected revenue

7. To estimate the total cost of the outsourcing project, including staff redundancy payments

Answer:

Option 1: This is a correct option. The decision maker should be fully briefed on the problem or opportunity addressed by the business case.

Option 2: This is a correct option. This is also known as the "do nothing" scenario and is a crucial element of a business case.

Option 3: This is an incorrect option. A business case should enable a non-technical decision maker to understand crucial technical information relating to the project.

Option 4: This is a correct option. The business case should propose a solution to a particular problem or opportunity.

Option 5: This is a correct option. The business case should outline how the project team intends to implement the plan.

Option 6: This is an incorrect option. The business case should provide an overview of a project for decision makers and for the project team, not for investors.

Option 7: This is a correct option. Estimates should include all personnel and financial resources needed to implement the project.

ELEMENTS OF A BUSINESS CASE

Elements of a business case

A business case is a document that defines your project and its goals. It helps you allocate resources, make provisions for unforeseen obstacles, and facilitate good decision making. The basic components in a business case include a current and pro forma balance sheet, an income statement, and a cash flow analysis.

A business case should answer some important questions about your proposed project:

- Why is the proposed solution needed, and what issues and opportunities does it address?
- What is the recommended solution to the issue or opportunity being addressed?
- What are the benefits of the proposed solution?
- What will happen to the business if the project is not undertaken?
- When will the solution be deployed?
- What human, financial, and time resources will be needed to deliver the solution?

Phil is an HR manager for a large software company. He's been working on an initiative for an improved records-management plan for the company. Phil believes that there's a pressing need for the organization to meet its legal and business obligations by improving access to records and information.

The senior executives in Phil's company require a detailed justification of Phil's business proposal before they will consider it. Phil has never drawn up a business case before, and needs to know what elements to include in the document.

A good business case must contain certain elements:

Background

The background outlines the business problem or opportunity that exists.

Executive summary

The executive summary is a short summary of the entire business case. It is presented first, but is usually written last.

Situational assessment and problem statement

The situational assessment and problem statement section contains detailed information about the problems or opportunities facing the organization.

Project description

The project description contains detailed information about the project. It should contain a description and scope for the project, as well as the project objectives.

Solution description

The solution description details the solution you are proposing to deal with the issues and opportunities detailed in the situational assessment. The solution description should give the concept overview, solution detail, sub-project structure, and solution alternatives.

The business case should also contain these key elements.

Cost and benefit analysis

The cost and benefit analysis gives a detailed analysis of the costs and benefits of implementing the proposed solution.

Implementation timeline

The implementation timeline shows the projected schedule for implementing the solution, and assures management that your team has thought about and accommodated any issues that may arise. Your implementation section should also address implementation components, major milestones, and major dependencies.

Critical assumptions and risk assessment

The critical assumptions and risk assessment section contains a list of the assumptions that have been used while developing a solution.

Conclusions and recommendations

The conclusions and recommendations section closes the business case. It should give a brief summary of the case's main points. It should convey a sense of urgency and remind the reader of the risks of not carrying out the proposed project.

In his business case for implementing an improved records-management plan for the company, Phil gives some background on the company's existing records system, noting that it has been in use since 2002. His situational assessment and problem statement section describes the issues facing the company's record-maintenance efforts. It details the business and legal implications of inefficient record retrieval.

Phil then sets out the scope and objectives of his proposed project. The project's main objective is to implement an improved system of records management via an updated database system. The solution description gives detailed information on the records management project, outlines a program for updating the records system, and indicates how the team will deal with the technical issues.

Phil's business case includes a preliminary analysis of the project's costs and benefits, including factors that may affect costs during implementation. He provides an outline schedule and development plan, including time and resource estimates for project tasks such as software upgrading and record conversion.

Phil details his main assumptions regarding present and future conditions that may affect the project's delivery. These include the renewal of the company's IT support contract and company policy on outsourcing. The conclusion sums up by reiterating the urgent need for an improved database system, and recommends that Phil's project be initiated without delay.

Question Set

Marsha is a project manager for a small Internet insurance firm. She hopes to set up a Customer Support Department, and is preparing to write a business case. She needs to know which are the crucial elements to incorporate before she begins.

Question 1 of 2

Question

Which of these elements should Marsha include to make her business case?

Options:

1. A description of the scope and objectives of the customer-support project
2. A statement of the problems facing the organization due to the lack of a customer-support service
3. A list of project assumptions made by Marsha and her team, and an evaluation of the risks involved in implementing the project
4. A list of accurate predictions of all obstacles that the project will encounter
5. A schedule for the development and rollout of the customer-support system
6. A detailed organization chart of all personnel involved in the project

Answer:

Option 1: This is a correct option. Marsha's project description should contain detailed project information, such as description, scope, and objectives.

Option 2: This is a correct option. The background section of the business case outlines the business problem or opportunity that exists.

Option 3: This is a correct option. The critical assumptions and risk assessment section contains a list of the assumptions that have been used while developing a solution.

Option 4: This is an incorrect option. It is impossible for Marsha to predict the specific issues that will arise, although she should outline how the team proposes to deal with unforeseen obstacles.

Option 5: This is a correct option. The implementation timeline shows Marsha's projected schedule for implementing the solution, and assures management that her team has thought about and addressed potential issues.

Option 6: This is an incorrect option. At this stage, the exact composition of the project team may be subject to change.

Question 2 of 2

Which of these elements should Marsha include in her case?

Options:

1. Detailed information on the need for the company to implement a customer-support service
2. A summary of the business case's main points and a recommendation to implement the proposed plan
3. A confidentiality agreement that must be signed by all readers of the business case
4. Details of how the customer-support service will deal with specified issues and opportunities
5. A detailed analysis of the costs and benefits of implementing the customer-support plan
6. An executive summary of the customer-support plan business case

Answer:

Option 1: This is a correct option. The situational assessment and problem statement section contains detailed information about the problems or opportunities facing the organization.

Option 2: This is a correct option. The conclusions and recommendations section enables Marsha to summarize the case's main points and remind the reader of the risks of not carrying out the project.

Option 3: This is an incorrect option. Unless the business case contains sensitive information, the normal confidentiality rules of the organization should suffice.

Option 4: This is a correct option. The solution description outlines the solution that Marsha's team recommends to deal with the issues and opportunities detailed in the situational assessment.

Option 5: This is a correct option. The cost and benefit analysis gives a detailed analysis of the costs and benefits of implementing the proposed solution.

Option 6: This is a correct option. The executive summary is a short summary of all information included in Marsha's business case, and is usually written last.

MARKETING COMPONENTS

Marketing components

When evaluating your business case, company decision makers are interested in how your proposed project intends to reach customers and create sales.

You present this information within the marketing components section of your business case. The business case should include five marketing components:

the research plan

The research plan details how your team intends to gather and analyze information about existing customer needs.

project features and benefits

The project features and benefits component outlines the features and benefits that the project will bring to the organization, such as increased inventory turnover, access to new customers, and reduced staffing levels.

the creative plan

The creative plan outlines how your team is going to inform customers about your product. This plan should be simple, memorable, and focused on the benefits of the proposal.

the marketing communications plan

The marketing communications plan details how time and money will be allocated to distributing product information to customers.

the sales plan

The sales plan communicates strategies for acquiring new business, growing existing business, and making or exceeding sales.

The marketing components of a business case are often interlinked and interdependent.

For example, advertising is a crucial component of any marketing communications plan. The ideas used in advertising are usually drawn up in your creative plan, which is itself dependent upon the customer needs described in your research plan.

Sergio is an online-sales manager for a large leisure travel company. Nearly 80% of the company's package sales are online, and the company's image is very Internet based. Sergio needs to present a business case for updating the online ordering system. The company executives are keen to know how this project will benefit the company.

In the marketing components section of his business case, Sergio proposes a survey of all customers to assess their online ordering habits and requirements. In the project features and benefits section, Sergio suggests that the proposed update will increase inventory turnover by up to 6% a year, and will help reach new customers.

Sergio's creative plan outlines strategies for advertising the new system, including special deals and a loyalty scheme for regular customers. His marketing communications plan suggests targeted advertising of products to repeat customers. And his sales plan aims to use different incentives to entice new business and retain existing customers.

With the help of good research and a well-defined set of product features and benefits, you can construct an effective creative plan, marketing communications plan, and sales plan. These components are crucial to a good business case, as they demonstrate to the decision makers that your team has considered the bottom line - that is, reaching customers and creating sales.

Question

Nancy is a marketing manager with an educational software company. She's constructing a business case for an "introduce a friend" promotional initiative that she believes will increase sales and reach new customers.

Identify the marketing components that should be included in Nancy's business case.

Options:

1. The technical specifications of the project
2. Plans for a customer-wide survey to find out which promotional initiative will be most successful
3. Details of how customer referrals can be used to expand the company's customer base
4. A plan for a customer-wide e-mail advertising campaign
5. The development timetable for the project
6. Details of the resources required to initiate the e-mail advertising campaign
7. Projections for how the referrals of existing customers will increase sales to new customers

Answer:

Option 1: This is an incorrect option. The technical specification is not a marketing-related component of the business case.

Option 2: This is a correct option. The research plan details how Nancy's team intends to gather and analyze information about existing customer needs.

Option 3: This is a correct option. The project features and benefits component outlines the features and benefits that the project will bring to the organization.

Option 4: This is a correct option. The creative plan outlines how Nancy's team is going to inform customers about the initiative.

Option 5: This is an incorrect option. The development timetable is not a marketing-related component of the business case.

Option 6: This is a correct option. The marketing communications plan details how time and money will be allocated to distributing product information to customers.

Option 7: This is a correct option. The sales plan communicates strategies for acquiring new business, growing existing business, and making or exceeding sales.

SECTION 2 - BEFORE WRITING A BUSINESS CASE

SECTION 2 - Before Writing a Business Case

Successful business cases are supported by three key processes: proposing, selecting, and tracking. Failure to implement effective business-case processes can have adverse effects on your business. Researching your business case thoroughly and aligning it with your company's business objectives makes it more likely to be selected by your company's decision makers.

In this lesson, you will find out what needs to be researched before writing a business case, and how to determine whether a proposed project aligns with corporate strategy. You will also learn how to determine the best angle for a business case, and how to identify the information that should be included.

Your organization's corporate strategy is of central importance to a new project. You need to ensure that your proposed project supports the company's overall strategic direction. If a project does not align with corporate strategy, the key decision makers will question the wisdom of the investment and, most likely, not approve it.

In order to establish whether a project is in alignment, you must first identify the actual applications and benefits that are offered by the proposed project. Then you need to familiarize yourself with the company's corporate strategy. A project may be said to align with the corporate strategy if the processes or practices supported by the project directly assist the organization in achieving its strategy.

Once you've verified that the project aligns with corporate strategy, you need to quantify the benefits of the project through an analysis of the impact of the proposed benefits on the operation of the business. This should be expressed in financial amounts.

Decision makers are the people who will decide whether your project is approved. Identifying the decision makers, defining their interest in your case, and finding answers to the kinds of questions they may ask will help you to prepare and present a strong business case. Different decision makers, such as company executives, stockholders, managers, and outside finance groups, have different expectations from business proposals.

In addition to the decision makers, many other individuals or groups will need to refer to your business case, for various reasons, throughout the project life cycle.

RESEARCHING YOUR PROJECT

Researching your project

An effective business case must be well written, interesting, to the point, and able to communicate a message to the reader effectively. Successful business cases are supported by three key processes:

proposing

The proposing process provides standards and methods for building and submitting good business cases.

selecting

The selecting process defines the decision makers and the process they use for funding projects.

tracking

The tracking process monitors the investment value of the project by comparing its actual value with that forecasted by the business case.

Sam, a project manager for a clothing company, is preparing a business case. With the key processes in place, Sam's business case benefits as follows:

proposing

Because he is following the proposing process set out by his company for preparing a good business case, Sam's proposal ensures that he will receive a fair hearing.

selecting

Sam identifies the key decision makers for business proposals in his company, and familiarizes himself with the process they use for approving funding for projects.

tracking

Sam includes in his business case a forecast of the value of the project, for comparison with its actual value when it is implemented.

Failure to implement effective business-case processes can have adverse effects on your company's business as well as on your business case.

Proposing

Failure to implement a defined proposing process can mean that investment proposals with high potential value are overlooked in favor of low-payoff options, because there is no process to encourage an accurate business-case analysis. The business then loses out on returns on investment.

Selecting

Without a good selection process, good business proposals may be ignored when politically powerful decision makers push through an inferior alternative option. The lack of consistent selection criteria results in good investment options being ignored.

Tracking

Failure to implement a tracking process can be detrimental when an approved project fails to meet its targets during implementation because its scope was modified during rollout. The new scope negated value assumptions outlined in the original business case, and the shortfall was not noticed in time to revise the project targets.

"Nicely written business case, John, but I've no idea how this proposed time-management system is going to affect productivity. And how much will it cost anyway?" It is pointless to write a business case unless it includes effective, pertinent, and useable information, and unless the proposal aligns with company objectives.

It's essential to research your business case thoroughly, so that all costs, benefits, assumptions, and potential constraints of the project are fully investigated.

If you research your business case well, and align it with business processes, you are more likely to:

- persuade decision makers that your project should be selected,
- secure the resources you need.

After the initial rejection of his business case, John decided that some extra research was needed. In particular, he looked at the costs and benefits associated with the time-management system. He tracked how the implementation of the system could be tied directly to the company's bottom line, and illustrated this in the business case.

John's business case was successful when he resubmitted it. He was awarded all the resources he required to implement the system, which significantly increased productivity in the company.

Question

Why is it important to research your business case and align it with business processes?

Options:

1. You will ensure significant benefits for the company
2. You are more likely to persuade decision makers that your project should be implemented
3. You will increase company productivity
4. You are more likely to secure the resources you need

Answer:

Option 1: This is an incorrect option. The benefits of a project to a company will become apparent only when the project is implemented.

Option 2: This is a correct option. Researching your business case enables you to answer questions regarding the costs, benefits, assumptions, and potential constraints of the project.

Option 3: This is an incorrect option. Your business case on its own will not boost productivity, but it can describe how a proposed project may do so.

Option 4: This is a correct option. A business case that includes effective, pertinent, and useable information, and that aligns with company objectives, is more likely to be approved for funding.

x

BACKGROUND INFORMATION

Background information

Naomi is a project manager for Red Rock Mountain Jeep Tours. This is a privately owned jeep-touring company based in Sedona, Arizona. The company is the market leader in the jeep-touring industry. She is preparing a business case for the expansion of her business's customer offering. She believes that this project, if implemented, will mean increased sales and a larger market share for the company.

To give her project the best chance of being approved, Naomi needs to carry out a certain amount of research before she starts writing her business case. Researching a business case involves investigating four key aspects of the project.

Benefits

You need to research the benefits that the project will bring to the organization, such as increased inventory turnover, access to new customers, and reduced staffing levels.

Costs

You need to research the resources and costs needed to implement the new project.

Assumptions

You need to research the assumptions being made about the company and the conditions in which the new project will be created.

Constraints

You need to research any factors that may limit the development of the project, such as budget and resource limitations or schedule restrictions.

Currently, Red Rock Mountain Jeep Tours simply rents jeeps to customers. Naomi believes that by looking after all its customers' travel arrangements and accommodation requirements for the duration of a vacation, the company can offer a more attractive product and drive up company earnings.

In order to research the project, Naomi needs to investigate

- the benefits that the new customer offering can bring to Red Rock Mountain Jeep Tours,
- the costs associated with changing their offering so customers' travel arrangements and accommodation requirements are catered to,
- the assumptions that she must make regarding the present and future of Red Rock Mountain Jeep Tours,
- any constraints that may limit the scope of the project, such as availability of staff in the area.

Question

What do you need to research before you start writing a business case?

Options:

1. Benefits
2. Staff
3. Costs
4. Outcome
5. Assumptions
6. Constraints

Answer:

Option 1: This is a correct option. You need to research the benefits that the project will bring to the company, such as increased inventory turnover, access to new customers, and reduced staffing levels.

Option 2: This is an incorrect option. It is not necessary to research staff before you begin to write a business case.

Option 3: This is a correct option. You need to research the resources and costs needed to implement the new project.

Option 4: This is an incorrect option. The outcome of the project is unknown at this stage.

Option 5: This is a correct option. You need to research the assumptions being made about the company and the conditions in which the new project will be created.

Option 6: This is a correct option. You need to research any factors that may limit the development of the project.

Project costs fall into a number of areas:

personnel costs

Personnel costs include costs for all personnel involved in the project, whether they are involved only for a short time or for the duration of the project. Examples of personnel costs include the design team, system test and implementation resources, and staff that are required during the operation of the project.

overhead for the project

Overhead expenses are costs that are incurred by the project personnel over the book of the project. These include facilities, supplies, travel, and any other personnel-related expenses.

consultant support

Consultant support covers the costs involved in hiring consultants to help with the project.

operational transition costs

Operational transition costs cover any changes in work practices caused by the proposed project. These costs could include productivity loss during transition, training expenses, and redundancy payments.

installation costs

Installation costs are the expenses incurred as a result of physical changes such as wiring or network installation.

outsourcing costs

Outsourcing costs are costs associated with moving work to other organizations outside the company.

Question

Identify areas that project costs fall into.

Options:

1. Personnel
2. Office insurance
3. Overhead
4. Litigation
5. Operational transition
6. Consultant support
7. Installation

Answer:

Option 1: This is a correct option. You need to assess personnel costs over the duration of the project.

Option 2: This is an incorrect option. Office insurance typically does not form part of project costs.

Option 3: This is a correct option. Overhead costs such as facilities and supplies expenses are incurred by personnel during a project.

Option 4: This is an incorrect option. Litigation costs do not form part of a project's costs.

Option 5: This is a correct option. Operational transition costs cover any changes in work practices caused by the proposed project.

Option 6: This is a correct option. You will need to pay fees to any consultants who help with the project.

Option 7: This is a correct option. Installation of networks and wiring, for example, will form part of project costs.

The categories of business case benefits include:

improved customer satisfaction

Improved customer satisfaction can result from changes to a business solution. For example, a new business solution can enhance customers' experience with your products and services.

increased revenue and market share

Many business changes can increase revenue and market share, or improve customer retention. If there is a direct link between a business change and an increase in revenue or market share, you can include these benefits in the financial return calculation of the business case. If there is no clear link, these improvements are categorized as qualitative benefits only.

improved employee satisfaction

New business processes can contribute to improved employee satisfaction. You can mention such improvements in the business case as qualitative benefits. Sometimes, employee satisfaction directly affects productivity and these improvements may be included in the operational benefits.

For your project to be a success, you must complete a cost and benefit analysis to establish whether

- all benefits are identified and quantified within the business solution,
- qualitative benefits are clarified and incorporated into the business solution,
- high-level benefits are authorized and all assumptions are approved by the relevant department,
- unproductive elements of the business case can be eliminated.

Cost analysis helps you to identify the costs associated with the implementation of your project and allow for any hidden costs. A cost and benefit analysis establishes whether the project is worthwhile. It is important to involve your organization in the analysis to help it prepare for the implementation process.

Unplanned changes to a project can invalidate even the most carefully planned cost analysis. Using the Activity-based Costing (ABC) model enables you to evaluate the impact on expenditure and revenue when changes occur to business processes. Resources and overhead costs are easily calculated using ABC, enabling you to see exactly how much is being spent on particular products and services.

Back at Red Rock Mountain Jeep Tours, Naomi sets her team to work on calculating the costs associated with the expanded customer travel and accommodation offering, in terms of:

personnel

The new approach requires specialized staff to deal with travel and accommodation bookings by phone and online. In addition, temporary design and development personnel will be needed to implement the technical side of the project.

overhead

The team will need sufficient computer facilities and support for the project, and some team members will need to travel to executive meetings to give project updates.

consultant support

Business and technical consultants will be needed to provide assistance implementing the new business model.

installation requirements

The new approach enables customers to book their vacation package online, so a reliable client/server-based e-commerce system must be installed.

Naomi's team calculates the potential benefits of the expanded customer travel package model in the areas of:

operational savings

The project will mean savings for the company because the online-booking facility reduces the need to maintain booking offices.

improved customer satisfaction

The ability of the company to provide a complete vacation-booking service to its customers will increase customer satisfaction.

increased revenue and market share

The project increases the company's market share by expanding its offerings to include complete vacation packages. This also attracts more revenue.

improved employee satisfaction

The new system makes employees' jobs easier. The new vacation package offering also enables commission-based sales representatives to increase their income.

Naomi's team then compares the costs and benefits to decide whether the customer travel package project is a worthwhile one for Red Rock Mountain Jeep Tours. Ultimately, Naomi's cost-benefit analysis concludes that the project is indeed worthwhile. The result of the analysis will be included in the business case.

Assumptions are explicit statements used to describe the present and future environment. When you are developing a business case, you usually need to make certain assumptions. All assumptions must be identified and documented in the business case, so the decision maker is familiar with the basis for alternatives.

Your business case must document certain assumptions about the proposed project. These assumptions should be tested with project stakeholders and operational managers before you include them in the business case. You need to discuss the strengths, weaknesses, opportunities, and threats (SWOT), as well as any risks associated with implementing the solution.

At Red Rock Mountain Jeep Tours, Naomi's team now needs to compile and document the assumptions associated with the customer travel package project. The team brainstorms the project assumptions, and tests them by discussing them with project stakeholders and operational managers. Any issues that are brought to light in these discussions are documented.

Constraints that can affect your project include:

- scheduling constraints,
- budget constraints,
- quality constraints,
- technical constraints.

Naomi's team needs to compile and document the constraints associated with the expanded customer travel and accommodation project. The team brainstorms the project constraints, and documents the constraints in each area:

budget

Naomi's project must fall within the limits of the departmental budget for new projects. The maximum available funding is $100,000.

quality

The scope of the project's proposed online system is constrained by the fact that not all the company's potential customers have broadband Internet or fast download capability.

scheduling

Naomi's project will involve some disruption of the company's existing services, so the project needs to be scheduled for low season to minimize any potential downtime.

technical

The technical requirements of the project must fit in with the existing company network.

Naomi's team tests the assumptions and constraints by discussing them with project stakeholders and operational managers at Red Rock Mountain Jeep Tours.

Any issues that are brought to light in these discussions are documented.

Case Study: Question 1 of 4

Scenario

You are researching a project proposal for a company called Zoflina, which provides products and documentation on good manufacturing process.

You want to develop a business case that documents the possibilities that are available to the company.

Questions may be answered in any order.

Question

Which costs will need to be researched for this project?

Options:

1. Installation costs
2. Personnel
3. Overhead
4. Consultant support

Answer:

Option 1: This is an incorrect option. Because the company already specializes in databases, the project does not require the installation of any new software.

Option 2: This is a correct option. The data-entry component of the project will require the hiring of temporary data-entry staff.

Option 3: This is a correct option. Visits to the company headquarters to give project updates will result in some travel costs.

Option 4: This is an incorrect option. This project does not require the input of a consultant.

Case Study: Question 2 of 4

Which benefits should be documented for this project?

Options:

1. Improved customer satisfaction
2. Operational savings
3. Increased revenue and market share
4. Improved employee satisfaction

Answer

Option 1: This is a correct option. The range of databases offered by Zoflina would increase, providing customers with a more diverse offering.

Option 2: This is an incorrect option. The move to increased devělopment of databases does not necessarily guarantee operational savings, although it will increase sales.

Option 3: This is a correct option. The increased range of databases would enable Zoflina to expand into new sectors.

Option 4: This is an incorrect option. The benefits of the project do not include improved employee satisfaction.

Case Study: Question 3 of 4

Who in the company can help you to research and test project assumptions?

Options:

1. Operational managers
2. Project team members
3. Executive directors
4. Project stakeholders
5. Customers

Answer:

Option 1: This is a correct option. In this case, the database development managers can provide useful information on the validity of project assumptions.

Option 2: This is a correct option. The project team has an indepth understanding of the requirements of the project, and can be used to research the assumptions.

Option 3: This is an incorrect option. Zoflina's executive directors are not sufficiently involved in the project to be of any help in testing project assumptions.

Option 4: This is a correct option. In this case, database development and marketing managers have a stake in the project and can help to test its assumptions.

Option 5: This is an incorrect option. Customers are not part of the company and are not direct stakeholders in the project.

Case Study: Question 4 of 4

Which constraints associated with the project should you document?

Options:

1. Scheduling constraints
2. Staff constraints
3. Budget constraints
4. Quality constraints
5. Technical constraints

Answer:

Option 1: This is a correct option. In this case, project implementation must take place during the summer months.

Option 2: This is an incorrect option. This project is not working under any staff constraints.

Option 3: This is a correct option. You cannot exceed the maximum allowable budget for the project.

Option 4: This is an incorrect option. There are no quality constraints for this project.

Option 5: This is a correct option. The project must use the existing technical structures in the company.

x

WHAT NEEDS TO BE RESEARCHED

What needs to be researched

It is important to research the costs, benefits, assumptions, and constraints associated with a project, and to include your findings in your business case. The decision makers who read your business case need this information in order to weigh the pros and cons of the project. You need to know how to identify and categorize the costs and benefits of your project.

To identify the costs associated with a project, you should:

form a team

Your cost-identification team should include the key members of the project team, to ensure a good understanding of the key issues associated with the project and the possible costs.

choose a facilitator

The facilitator should be someone who can remain impartial and help the group to reach agreement on any issues that may arise.

identify the costs

It is useful to create a list of possible costs for comparison with the costs actually incurred over the book of the project. Unquantifiable costs should be noted and mentioned in your cost discussion in the business case.

enter the costs in a spreadsheet

You should organize the spreadsheet according to a relevant time period, such as a year, quarter, or month, with a column for each unit of time over the expected project duration. The subtotals of the costs of each project element for each period are added up to give the total cost.

Ana is a project manager for an educational software company. She wants to investigate a new system that will make the company's product database more efficient. She wants to carry out some research on the issue before she begins work on a business case.

To identify the costs associated with the project, Ana:

forms a team

Ana's cost-identification team consists of members of the project team who are familiar with the product database, the development technologies that will be used, and what the proposed update would involve.

chooses a facilitator

Ana asks Bob, a software developer from outside the project team, to perform the role of facilitator, as he can provide impartial judgment on project-related issues.

creates a list of possible costs

The main costs of the project are those incurred during a database cleanup, software purchase and installation, server upgrade, and the hiring of an IT consultant.

enters the costs into a spreadsheet

Ana's team organizes the cost data on a monthly basis, to coincide with the main project milestones.

Question

Alan, a project manager at an IT company, is putting a business case together for an online marketing campaign. Alan needs to identify the project costs. In which order should he take these steps?

Options:

A. List the costs of designing advertisements and displaying them on major portal sites

B. Ask Jane, the accounts manager, to sit in on discussions

C. Input into a spreadsheet all research, development, and execution costs for the campaign, arranged by quarter

D. Create a team, including marketing personnel, a graphic designer, and an IT consultant, to discuss costs

Answer:

Create a team, including marketing personnel, a graphic designer, and an IT consultant, to discuss costs is ranked as the first step. Your cost-identification team should include the key members of the project team, to ensure a good understanding of the key issues associated with the project and the possible costs.

Ask Jane, the accounts manager, to sit in on discussions is ranked as the second step. You should choose a facilitator who can remain impartial and help the group to reach agreement on any issues that may arise.

List the costs of designing advertisements and displaying them on major portal sites is ranked as the third step. You should create a list of possible costs for comparison with the costs actually incurred over the book of the project.

Input into a spreadsheet all research, development, and execution costs for the campaign, arranged by quarter is ranked as the fourth step. You should organize the spreadsheet according to a relevant time period, such as a year, quarter, or month, with a column for each unit of time over the expected project duration.

Once you've documented the costs of the project, you need to identify the benefits of the project.

Your benefit-analysis team should include key members of the project team so that everyone has a common understanding of the benefits, and how they are linked to the original project objectives. The team should have a facilitator. Your team should brainstorm the benefits that your organization will gain from your project, so that no potential benefit is overlooked.

Benefits should highlight tangible returns in terms of cost savings and incremental revenue, but qualitative benefits, such as increased customer satisfaction and employee satisfaction, should also be included. You should include stakeholders and operational managers in this process, to foster cross- organizational support for the business case.

When you have compiled a list of benefits, you should categorize them into natural groups, combining similar areas and eliminating any redundancies. Once you've done this, you can compare these benefits with the original objectives for the project and identify any gaps and oversights. This enables you to align the benefits with the project objectives.

Question

Identify the steps you should take to identify benefits of a project.

Options:

1. Choose a team and facilitator
2. Have a meeting to discuss all ideas for potential benefits
3. Consider only tangible project benefits
4. List the benefits
5. Identify any gaps or oversights
6. Keep the process strictly within the team

Answer:

Option 1: This is a correct option. Your team should include key members of the project team so that everyone has a common understanding of the benefits.

Option 2: This is a correct option. Your team should brainstorm the benefits that your organization will gain from your project, so that no potential benefit is overlooked.

Option 3: This is an incorrect option. Qualitative benefits, such as increased customer satisfaction and employee satisfaction, should also be considered.

Option 4: This is a correct option. You should categorize the list of benefits into natural groups, combining similar areas and eliminating any redundancies.

Option 5: This is a correct option. Comparing the benefits with the original objectives for the project enables you to align the benefits with the project objectives.

Option 6: This is an incorrect option. You should include stakeholders and operational managers in the process, to foster cross-organizational support for the business case.

Having documented the costs of her project, Ana needs to identify the project benefits. She begins by putting together a benefits-identifying team with a facilitator. The team meets and brainstorms potential benefits of the project. Increased database efficiency brings the tangible benefits of increased revenue and possibly more new business.

The new database also brings qualitative benefits such as greater time savings for employees and improved customer service. These are then aligned with the main project objectives of helping product managers and sales staff to work more efficiently and increase sales. It is vital that your business case documents any assumptions that are made concerning the project. You should examine your assumptions in three main categories.

Product

Product assumptions relate to the product or service being offered by the project. Questions to be asked include: Does the project meet customer needs? Will it have a measurable impact on the company's bottom line? Are the costs prohibitive? Are the necessary materials easily obtainable? Are the product support systems established? Can the product be developed in a reasonable amount of time?

Economic

Economic assumptions relate to the economic environment in which your project will operate. Questions you should ask are: Is your industry currently healthy? How do economic changes affect your industry? Are your industry forecasts positive?

Market

Market assumptions are those that concern the potential market for the project. You should ask: Is the market for your product or service clearly identifiable? Is the market ready for your idea? Is the market large enough to support your idea? What barriers are there to entering your market?

To answer the many practical questions that will arise when documenting project assumptions, you should work with people who are actively involved at an operational level.

Managers and consultants, for example, have the expertise to help you test project assumptions. Company directors, on the other hand, are more concerned with broad strategic issues than with the requirements of specific projects.

Having researched the costs and benefits for the database project, Ana meets with John, a sales manager, and Ravi, the company's IT manager, to discuss the project assumptions.

Ana: For this business case I'm making the assumption that there is a real business need for improved access to our product catalogue. Can you back me up on this John?

John: I certainly can. We're losing a lot of business by not having ready access to our product offerings. Our sales staff have been looking to get this issue resolved for a long time.

Ana: OK, good. Ravi, I'm assuming that existing IT support systems will be sufficient to allow the database project to roll out in a reasonable amount of time. Does that seem fair?

Ravi: That shouldn't be a problem - we can provide support for the database cleanup, software installation, and server upgrade. But you'll have to budget for any additional resources.

John: Speaking of costs, we should also assume that sales over the next quarter will remain constant. This will be important when calculating the impact of any downtime.

Ana: Yes, I'll take this into consideration. Finally, I'm assuming that the market conditions for this project are as good as they're going to get, and that it should be done right away. What do you think?

John: I think that's right. We've reached a point where our sales figures are falling behind, because the product information just isn't accessible. If we don't do something about it, we'll be overtaken by the competition.

Ravi: John and I have worked together on the requirements, and the demand for the project is very high - from both employees and customers.

Ana has tested the assumptions of the business case with Ravi and John, both of whom are stakeholders in the project. In doing this, she ensures the validity of her assumptions, and also gains support for the project across different departments. It is important to document and validate all assumptions, and to keep track of the sources you use for statistics and cost estimates.

Question

Which steps should you take to test assumptions for your project?

Options:

1. Examine product assumptions
2. Discuss them with project stakeholders and operational managers
3. Examine the company's past activity

4. Discuss them with the board of directors
5. Examine economic assumptions
6. Examine market assumptions

Answer:

Option 1: This is a correct option. You need to decide whether the product or service meets customer needs, how it will affect the company's bottom line, if it is viable in terms of cost and resources, and if it can be realized in a reasonable amount of time.

Option 2: This is a correct option. This helps to foster cross-organizational support for the project.

Option 3: This is an incorrect option. Assumptions are statements used to describe the present and future environment, not the past.

Option 4: This is an incorrect option. The board of directors is not sufficiently engaged with the project to be able to test your assumptions.

Option 5: This is a correct option. You should examine the economic environment in which your industry is situated, and try to anticipate changes.

Option 6: This is a correct option. This helps you to establish whether the proposed market is identifiable, of sufficient size, and ready for the product or service.

Constraints limit the scope and content of available alternative solutions. To research the constraints on a project, you should talk to team members to determine the likely availability of resources.

You should also consider your company's corporate culture, and the positive or negative effects that your proposed project could have on the company and its employees. Finally, you need to list and prioritize the criteria for the project, as they relate to the constraints.

For example, you may need to rank criteria such as schedule, cost, and quality in order of importance.

Ana and her team are researching the constraints affecting the database project. To do this, the team must:

research the availability of resources

The project will require some IT support during implementation, as well as the hiring of temporary staff.

investigate the corporate culture

The team reviews the company's rules, methods, and procedures for the business areas affected by the project.

list the schedule and budget constraints

The departmental budget for new projects is $70,000. The project needs to be completed before the start of the next financial quarter.

list the quality constraints

The product database needs to be accessed by customers, so it may need to contain more information relating to purchase price, shipping charges, and sales tax than one developed solely for employee use.

list the technical constraints

The database needs upgrading, and new software and hardware need to be integrated into the existing system.

prioritize the constraints

Ana's team decides that the schedule constraint should be prioritized over budgetary, technical, and quality constraints.

Question

Which steps should be carried out when investigating project constraints?

Options:

1. Research the availability of resources
2. Investigate the corporate culture

3. Research the competition

4. List the schedule, budget, quality, and technical constraints

5. Prioritize the constraints

6. Plan the project outside the constraints

Answer

Option 1: This is a correct option. You should discuss the issue of resources with members of your project team to assess availability.

Option 2: This is a correct option. This helps you to consider the positive or negative effects that your project could have on the company and its employees.

Option 3: This is an incorrect option. The competition does not affect the project's constraints.

Option 4: This is a correct option. These are constraints that directly affect the implementation and delivery of your project.

Option 5: This is a correct option. For example, you may need to rank criteria such as schedule, cost, and quality in order of importance.

Option 6: This is an incorrect option. Constraints dictate the parameters of your project, so it is not possible to work outside them.

Simon is a sales manager at a national bookstore, with 79 branches throughout the United States. He wants to put together a business case for a supplier extranet web site to make ordering more efficient and streamline the supply and ordering processes across the stores. The categories that Simon researches are:

costs

Simon forms a team with personnel from different branches, and chooses a business acquaintance as a facilitator. He outlines and records all costs associated with development of the extranet, from planning through to rollout and training.

benefits

Simon forms a team from members of his project team, and a facilitator from outside the team. The team lists the benefits to the company of the extranet project - for example a more integrated ordering process and increased customer satisfaction.

assumptions

Simon tests the project's assumptions by discussing them with sales and development personnel. He is assuming that the project can be completed within a reasonable time frame, that the costs will not run over budget, and that the current demand in stores for the extranet system will continue.

constraints

Simon researches the availability of resources for the project, the corporate culture, and the schedule, budget, quality, and technical constraints. Because the extranet ordering system needs to be rolled out quickly and seamlessly, the schedule constraint takes priority over budget or technical constraints.

Case Study: Question 1 of 4

Scenario

Omar is a project manager in a successful clothing company. He is researching the costs, benefits, assumptions, and constraints of a project before writing the business case.

Use the Learning Aid Omar's Project to get background information on the project. Then select the best methods for researching the information required for his case.

Questions may be answered in any order.

Question

Which steps should Omar take to identify costs?

Options:

1. Research all the costs by himself

2. Form a cost-identification team with members of his project team and IT personnel

3. Ask Lionel, a colleague of Omar's from the HR Department, to be the team facilitator

4. List the costs of hiring a dedicated web administrator, developing a new web site, and upgrading the web security software

5. Create a list of unquantifiable costs such as those arising from possible changes to the project goals

6. Enter into a spreadsheet all costs associated with the research, development, and execution of the campaign by financial year

Answer:

Option 1: This is an incorrect option. Omar by himself would not have a sufficient overview of all the cost-related issues of the project.

Option 2: This is a correct option. This ensures a good understanding of the key issues and potential costs.

Option 3: This is a correct option. The facilitator should be someone who is not part of the project team and who can make impartial judgments.

Option 4: This is a correct option. The list of possible costs for setting up the project will be checked against the actual costs incurred over the book of the project.

Option 5: This is an incorrect option. At this stage, unquantifiable costs are not listed. However, they should be discussed in the business case.

Option 6: This is a correct option. Because the project is scheduled over the financial year, the spreadsheet should arrange costs by financial year.

Case Study: Question 2 of 4

Identify the areas in which Omar followed the correct procedure to identify the benefits of the project.

Options:

1. Forming a benefits-analysis team
2. Listing the cost savings of $40,000 per annum represented by the project
3. Listing customer satisfaction as a benefit
4. Keeping the entire process inside the team
5. Associating increased sales and cost savings with increased customer satisfaction and ordering efficiency

Answer:

Option 1: This is a correct option. Omar formed a team from key members of the project team, who have a common understanding of the benefits.

Option 2: This is a correct option. Omar's team has researched the tangible benefits of the project.

Option 3: This is an incorrect option. Omar's team listed only tangible benefits such as sales increases. Intangible benefits should also be included in a business case.

Option 4: This is an incorrect option. Omar should have included IT and sales managers in the process, to foster cross-organizational support for the business case.

Option 5: This is an incorrect option. Omar did not draw a connection between the financial benefits of the project and the qualitative benefits.

Case Study: Question 3 of 4

Identify the ways in which Omar's team correctly researched assumptions for the project.

Options:

1. By ascertaining the readiness of customers for the new web site
2. By discussing the assumptions with sales managers
3. By discussing the assumptions with marketing managers
4. By studying the financial forecasts

Answer:

Option 1: This is an incorrect option. Without the assistance of marketing staff, the team was unable to validate this market assumption.

Option 2: This is a correct option. This helped the team to validate its economic assumption.

Option 3: This is an incorrect option. The team did not discuss its assumptions with Marketing.

Option 4: This is a correct option. This may help the team to anticipate the future economic environment in relation to the project.

Case Study: Question 4 of 4

Which of these actions by Omar's team were effective in investigating the project constraints?

Options:

1. Establishing the availability of IT support for the project
2. Investigating the company's corporate culture

3. De-emphasizing the budget and quality constraints of the project

4. Prioritizing the timely rollout of the web site

5. Discussing the hiring of a web administrator

Answer:

Option 1: This is a correct option. Good IT support is necessary for the success of the project.

Option 2: This is an incorrect option. The impact of the project on other areas, such as corporate culture, was not considered by the team.

Option 3: This is a correct option. Project budget and quality issues were deemed subordinate to schedule constraints.

Option 4: This is a correct option. The schedule constraint is prioritized over the quality constraint, in response to feedback from Sales.

Option 5: This is an incorrect option. The hiring of the web administrator is a budgetary constraint, and has not been researched.

ALIGNING CORPORATE STRATEGY

Aligning corporate strategy

A company's strategy is the plan of action it uses to allocate resources in order to achieve its long-term goals. Your organization's corporate strategy is of central importance to a new project. You need to ensure that your proposed project does not go against the company's overall strategic direction.

Mismatches between corporate and project strategies are a major cause of project failure. All companies have a strategy, whether it is explicit or implicit. Some organizations devote a lot of resources to formulating their strategy in written form, while others simply act out their strategy and do not articulate it.

A company's strategy integrates the company's major goals, policies, and actions into a coherent whole. A strategy responds to the needs of an organization in terms of its:

resources

A well-formed strategy helps to allocate an organization's resources to its advantage, taking into account the organization's competencies and shortcomings, anticipated changes in the business environment, and competitive activity.

external concerns

Strategic decisions are primarily concerned with external, rather than internal, issues. Most importantly, strategic decisions need to address and influence what the company produces and the markets to which it will sell.

The Managec Group, a retailer of electronic components, has a very customer-focused corporate strategy. The company deals with only high-quality manufacturers that offer complementary product lines. This enables Managec to offer customers both variety and consistency in the components they purchase.

Managec aims to accomplish customer and revenue growth by increasing sales volume on particular product lines. A key part of Managec strategy is its sales team, who provide product expertise and a comprehensive customer-support service. In the long term, Managec expects to achieve growth organically and by creating partnerships in key geographic markets.

New processes and practices created by a project need to support the corporate strategy. They must be in alignment with it, rather than work against it. If a project does not align with corporate strategy, the key decision makers will question the wisdom of the investment and, most likely, not approve it.

Best practice for aligning with corporate strategy

In order to establish whether a project is in alignment, you must first identify the actual applications and benefits that are offered by the proposed project. Then you must familiarize yourself with the company's corporate strategy. If the processes or practices supported by your project directly assist the organization in effecting its strategy, then the project is aligned. Finally, you need to quantify the benefits of the project through an analysis of the impact of the proposed benefits on the operation of the business.

Projects involving new or enhanced processes can benefit an organization in a number of areas.

Group productivity

Projects involving group productivity tools can increase the efficiency of all or part of an organization. Applications delivering this type of benefit include accounting systems, workflow systems, and inventory and production-management systems.

Individual or personal productivity

New processes supported by individual or personal productivity tools can enhance the efficiency of individual employees. Examples of applications delivering this type of benefit are spreadsheets, word-processing, and graphics packages.

Business activities productivity

Projects that promote time and space efficiency in business activities can have extensive benefits for an organization. They can often directly increase sales or reduce costs by, for example, reducing the need for office space. These projects often involve applications such as workflow systems, e-mail and Internet-based communication, and scheduling systems.

Having ascertained your organization's corporate strategy, and developed a list of applications and benefits that the project can bring to the company, the next step is to determine if these are in alignment.

A project may be said to align with the corporate strategy if the processes or practices supported by the project directly assist the organization in achieving its strategy. If a particular aspect of the corporate strategy is not addressed by the project, this does not mean that the project does not align. But a project should not work against any aspect of the corporate strategy.

The final step in the process is to quantify identified benefits in terms of financial amounts.

This process should include an analysis of the impact of the proposed benefit on the operation of the business. This involves an examination of the business process or practice that will be affected by the project. This enables you to predict the effect that the project will have on the organization's cost structure or income.

Suppose you are preparing a business case for a new e-procurement system for Managec, a retailer of electronic components. To ensure that the project aligns with corporate strategy, you need to:

make a list of the applications and benefits of the project

The e-procurement system provides a streamlined and efficient method of obtaining goods and services. Benefits of this system include increased savings on purchases, improved timeliness of the purchasing process, reduced waste, and improved supply-chain efficiency.

establish whether the applications and benefits of the project align with the corporate strategy

The efficiency of the e-procurement system means Managec can always get the right product at the right price and the right time. This aligns with Managec's customer-focused corporate strategy, which emphasizes excellent customer service.

quantify identified benefits in terms of financial amounts

The cost savings that accrue from a more efficient procurement system are easily quantifiable. The project may also mean quantifiable increases in Managec's sales income as a result of improved customer service and product availability.

Question

Philip is preparing a business case that proposes that employees should be able to work remotely, and outlines the infrastructure required to make this possible. He must ensure that the business case aligns with corporate strategy. How can he do this?

Options:

1. By identifying how the remote working will benefit the company
2. By indicating how the increased productivity and employee satisfaction accruing from the project can advance the company's goals
3. By listing the potential drawbacks of remote working, such as the lack of social contact and communication among employees
4. By quantifying the benefits by reviewing the savings involved in the reduced need for office space, lower staff turnover, and increased productivity
5. By outlining the available resources for the project, which includes his R&D team members

Answer:

Option 1: This is a correct option. Projects involving new or enhanced processes can benefit an organization in a number of areas.

Option 2: This is a correct option. A project may be said to align with the corporate strategy if the processes or practices supported by the project directly assist the organization in effecting its strategy.

Option 3: This is an incorrect option. Aligning the project with corporate strategy involves aligning the benefits, not the drawbacks.

Option 4: This is a correct option. This should be expressed in terms of financial amounts.

Option 5: This is an incorrect option. This does not help you to determine whether the project aligns with corporate strategy.

Trey, a manager in an IT company, is carrying out the research for a business case. His proposal is to create an IT help desk. Trey first talks to his manager, Amanda, to see if his project is in alignment with the corporate strategy. Then he discusses with Alan, a project team member, how to align the project with this strategy.

Trey: I'm researching this new project, and I just wanted to check with you to make sure I'm up to date on the company's corporate strategy.

Amanda: Well, our strategy is to offer a comprehensive product and service to our customers, and to expand our operation as much as possible. A key part of our strategy is follow-up and customer service. That's what makes us unique. You need to discuss this further with Alan.

Trey: An IT help desk would speed up our response to technical issues across the organization, and enable us to offer a better service to employees with IT problems. This would result in less employee downtime and greater productivity.

Alan: I can see the benefits to the company of this project. But we need to be clear about how the project will assist the company in achieving its strategy.

Trey: Well, follow-up and customer service are key parts of the corporate strategy, and we've calculated that a good IT help-desk system will reduce support-staff downtime by up to 15%. That will improve the level of customer service and follow-up.

Alan: Yes, we estimated that the resulting repeat business and word-of-mouth new business could mean a 20% increase in sales revenue.

Trey: Also, an expanded operation means more staff and potentially more IT problems. The help-desk system will help the IT Department to cope with this extra workload more efficiently, with minimal outlay in terms of equipment or additional staffing.

Alan: Yes, we've worked out that the project's effect on IT support processes will save the company up to $100,000 a year in IT costs, as well as generating the increased sales revenue.

Trey: Great, it looks like our project aligns with the company's strategy.

By checking with Amanda, Trey was able to familiarize himself with the main points of the company's corporate strategy. He was then able to compare these points with the benefits of the project.

Trey and Alan discussed how the benefits aligned with the corporate strategy, focusing on the new help- desk system and its predicted effect on sales revenue and IT costs. They quantified these benefits in financial terms.

They concluded that the project could directly assist the organization in achieving its strategy.

Case Study: Question 1 of 4

Scenario

You have been asked for advice by Neil, a project manager with a telecommunications company. Neil is preparing a business case but is unsure if the proposed project aligns with corporate strategy.

Answer the questions in sequence.

Question

Identify the benefits Neil's proposed project offers to the company.

Options:

1. Improved customer access to documentation
2. Improved documentation standards
3. Improved employee knowledge of the products
4. Company-wide employee satisfaction
5. Improved customer service

Answer:

Option 1: This is an incorrect option. The site is accessible to employees only.

Option 2: This is a correct option. The system enables product developers to perform regular updates,

which are instantly accessible to sales staff.

Option 3: This is a correct option. Sales staff can keep up to date with developments in products.

Option 4: This is an incorrect option. The project does not benefit employees outside sales and product development.

Option 5: This is a correct option. The documentation site enables sales staff to offer better service to their customers.

Case Study: Question 2 of 4

Identify the elements of the company's corporate strategy.

Options:

1. To provide a comprehensive, one-size-fits-all product
2. To position itself at the cutting edge of telecommunications technology
3. To provide regular product updates
4. To prioritize expanding into new markets over maintaining existing ones

Answer:

Option 1: This is an incorrect option. The company's strategy is to provide a base product that can be augmented and customized with a range of peripherals.

Option 2: This is a correct option. The company's frequent product updates are part of this strategy.

Option 3: This is a correct option. Updating the products is a key part of the company's strategy.

Option 4: This is an incorrect option. Good communication with existing customers is an equally important part of the corporate strategy.

Case Study: Question 3 of 4

Neil asks you if you think the project aligns with the company strategy. How do you answer?

Options:

1. "Yes, the project aligns with company strategy"
2. "No, the project does not align with company strategy"

Answer:

Option 1: This is a correct option. The company's strategy is to provide a base product that can be augmented and customized with a range of peripherals. Neil's proposed project supports this strategy.

Option 2: This is an incorrect option. Neil's proposed internal sales intranet supports the company's strategy by making information quickly available to sales staff, who will channel it to customers.

Case Study: Question 4 of 4

Identify the areas in which the corporate strategy and project benefits are in alignment.

Options:

1. Improved employee knowledge of the products
2. Market expansion
3. Improved access to information
4. Communication with customers

Answer:

Option 1: This is a correct option. This enhances customer service as well as facilitating follow-up sales.

Option 2: This is an incorrect option. The project does not affect the company's plans for market expansion.

Option 3: This is a correct option. This improves productivity among sales staff.

Option 4: This is a correct option. Customers who have previously bought the company's products are kept informed about new updates.

THE BEST ANGLE

The best angle

A business case is written to provide company decision makers with the data they need to determine the viability of investment in your project. In order to convey your message effectively, it's worth devoting some time to researching the people to whom the case will be presented.

When researching the people who will decide whether your project is approved, you need to ask three questions:

- Who are the decision makers for my case?
- What are their interests in my case?
- What questions will they ask?

Your first question should be: **Who are the decision makers for your case?**

Depending on the project and the company, the key decision makers could be company owners and executives, corporate directors, or stockholders. They could also be research and development teams, sales and marketing teams, financial services and accounting teams, or banks and outside funding sources.

If your company is relatively small, the owners or partners may be the decision makers. In large companies, decisions may be made by a division president instead of the CEO or chairperson.

Question

Identify the meaning of the term "decision makers" from a list of possible definitions.

Options:

1. The people who decide what goes into your business case
2. The people who will decide whether your proposed project is approved for investment
3. The people who refer to your business case throughout the life cycle of the project

Answer

Option 1: This is an incorrect option. You and your team decide what goes into your business case, but you are not the decision makers.

Option 2: This is a correct option. Examples of decision makers are company executives, directors, managers, and marketing and development staff.

Option 3: This is an incorrect option. Your business case may be referred to by different groups throughout the project cycle, but they are not all decision makers.

Your second question should be: What are their interests in your case?

Some decision makers may read only the executive summary to see whether your idea has merit, while others may focus on the business-case presentation. Decision makers' professional interests often influence what they look for in a business case. Accounting personnel may go directly to the financial reports to look at the profit and expense projections. Sales and marketing personnel may be interested only in whether there is a market for your idea.

The third question you should ask is: What questions will the decision makers ask? Examples of questions that you may have to answer include the following:

- How will the product or service be promoted and priced?
- Does a market exist for the product or service, and is the market ready?
- How will customer service be handled?
- What are the labor requirements for the project?
- Is the budget for the project realistic?
- What materials will be needed for the project?
- Are these materials readily available?
- Are the current facilities sufficient to implement the project?

Identifying the decision makers, defining their interest in your case, and finding answers to the kinds of questions they may ask will help you to prepare and present a strong business case. Your research in these three areas will help to ensure the approval of your new proposal.

Question

How do you go about identifying the angle a business case should take?

Options:

1. Identify the decision makers
2. Identify the decision makers' interests in your case
3. Offer incentives to individual decision makers to induce them to approve your project
4. Identify the questions the decision makers may ask
5. Include only positive information in the business case

Answer:

Option 1: This is a correct option. There are different decision makers for different projects and different company structures.

Option 2: This is a correct option. Decision makers' professional interests often influence what they look for in a business case.

Option 3: This is an incorrect option. You will not influence the decision makers by trying to bribe them.

Option 4: This is a correct option. The decision makers' questions will depend on their specific interests in your case.

Option 5: This is an incorrect option. Your business case should provide decision makers with all the data they need to determine the viability of investment in your project.

Decision makers are probably the most important audience for your business case, as they have the final say on whether the project is approved for funding.

But other individuals or groups will also need to refer to your business case for a variety of reasons. They may need to refer to the case to stay focused, to check their own involvement in the case, and to explain the concept to new managers if there is a management change during project development.

To secure commitment and funding for a new product or service, it's important to present your business case effectively to the decision makers.

But bear in mind that the audience for your business case is not restricted to decision makers alone. Different groups and individuals will need to refer to your business case throughout the life cycle of the project.

ADDRESSING THE CONCERNS OF DECISION MAKERS

Addressing the concerns of decision makers

When you are preparing a business case, you must include the information that is relevant to, and will influence, the decision makers. Different decision makers have different expectations from business proposals.

Company executives want to know how a new product or service fits into their industry - whether it is related to the industry or opens up another direction. These concepts are known as:

vertical integration

Vertical integration occurs when a company expands into a related business. An example would be a coffee company that wholesales coffee to retail outlets, and then decides to open its own retail outlets.

horizontal integration

Horizontal integration occurs when a company seeks to sell different types of a single product to different markets. An example of horizontal integration is a clothing company that runs different retail outlets for both "luxury" and "price-conscious" clothing markets.

Company owners and executives need to know whether the cost of developing a new product will be offset by the eventual profits.

They must commit to the new product to the extent that they will approve the costs.

Corporate directors and stockholders must commit to new product development. They will have some of the same questions as owners and other company executives, such as

- How will the company stock be affected?
- What will be the cost?
- How will the cost affect stock dividends?

Marketing and development personnel can provide information for your business case, and can facilitate its approval through their commitment to the idea.

Marketing

Marketing personnel can help you determine whether a market exists for the product or service, and whether the market is ready for it. They can also provide information on promotion and pricing.

Development

Research and development staff can help to develop and modify the product prototype, help establish costs, identify possible production problems, and show commitment to the new product idea.

Some companies, depending on their size and financial situation, need to secure outside investment to support new product development. If this is true of your company, you may need to present your business case to bankers and other financial resource managers, such as venture capitalists.

These outside groups must commit to your new product or service idea. The business case helps them to determine whether your idea is a high or low risk for a loan. By considering the needs of these key groups and engaging them in the process, you can prepare an effective business case that helps you to secure the commitment and funding you need for your project.

Ravi is preparing a business case for the establishment of a new e-commerce site. He needs to influence a number of decision makers.

CEO

Ravi positions the e-commerce project as horizontally integrated into the existing business. He assures the CEO that, although the initial cost of the project is high, this will be offset by significantly increased sales revenue within a year.

Company marketing director

Ravi focuses on the cost of the e-commerce project, and states that the increased sales and raised profile resulting from the new ordering service will have a positive effect on the share price.

Marketing and development managers

Ravi focuses on the ripeness of the market for the new ordering service, and is able to confirm that the production resources for the project exist or can be made available.

By focusing on the key decision makers and their concerns, Ravi was successful in communicating how his project could benefit their particular areas of interest.

Alan works for an IT company, and he needs to persuade several decision makers in the company to approve his proposal for a new corporate intranet.

CEO

Alan does not convince the CEO because he gives no indication of how the corporate intranet will be integrated into the business, or how much it will cost.

Stock holders

Alan makes no connection between the implementation of a corporate intranet and the overall profitability or share price of the company.

Marketing and development team managers

Alan fails to give any information on the marketing potential for the corporate intranet project, or whether the necessary development resources are available.

Because Alan did not use his business case to address the specific concerns of the decision makers, he failed to convince the decision makers that his project was worth implementing.

SECTION 3 - WRITING AND DESIGNING A BUSINESS CASE

SECTION 3 - Writing and Designing a Business Case

Writing a business case involves more than just inserting information into a document. Good writing and design in your business case can help you to ensure that the business case is read, your message is conveyed effectively to its audience, and the information that you want to emphasize is, in fact, emphasized.

In this lesson, you will learn how to identify who on your team should be involved in writing your business case. You will find out how best to organize the content of the business case, and how to identify the most appropriate writing style. You will also learn about layout and design considerations for the finished business case.

To ensure a broad range of perspectives, everyone on your project team should be involved in the development of the business case. However, only one or two people should actually write the business case itself. The business-case writers should be members of the project team, have an overall understanding of the project, and be able to synthesize all the team's contributions into one document.

Keeping the number of writers to a minimum ensures a consistent style throughout the document.

It's important to use the right layout, typeface, and cover for your business case. A well-designed and professional-looking business case creates a positive impression and tells company decision makers that you have done your homework.

Correct use of white space, paragraphs, formatting, and typeface in your business case makes the content easier to read and helps draw attention to the important points. Binding your business case in a good-quality cover enhances the professional look of the document.

GOOD WRITING AND DESIGN

Good writing and design

The way you write and design your business-case document can influence how it is received by your company's decision makers.

"I think we're all in agreement that this business case is really well-written and very clear." Writing a business case involves more than just dumping information into a document. The production of a good business-case document involves designating the writer or writers, organizing the content, and implementing layout and design guidelines for the finished document.

Naomi, the project manager at Red Rock Mountain Jeep Tours, has completed the necessary research for her business case, and is now ready to begin writing. To produce the business-case document, Naomi must first designate the writer or writers of the business case. The writers then need to decide how to organize the content, and how the business case is to be laid out and designed.

Good writing and design in your business case can help you to:

- ensure that the business case is read,
- convey your message effectively to your audience,
- emphasize the information that you want to emphasize.

Because Naomi's team presented a well-designed and well-written business case to the company decision makers, her proposal was received favorably. She secured the funding that she needed for her project.

Question

Why is it important to use good writing and design in your business case?

Options:

1. To ensure that the business case is read
2. To make it look better researched
3. To convey your message effectively to its audience
4. To guarantee funding for your project
5. To emphasize the information that you want to emphasize

Answer:

Option 1: This is a correct option. Decision makers typically receive a lot of business cases, so it's worth making sure that your case looks readable and interesting.

Option 2: This is an incorrect option. There's no substitute for researching your business case, but good presentation makes it easier to read.

Option 3: This is a correct option. A well-designed, well-written business case conveys your message more effectively than a badly presented case.

Option 4: This is an incorrect option. Good writing and design help a business case to succeed, but they do not of themselves guarantee success.

Option 5: This is a correct option. You can write and design a business case to highlight important information.

WHO SHOULD BE INVOLVED

Who should be involved

Jan, a financial manager in an architectural firm, is working on a business case for an improved payroll system. She and her team have done the necessary research, aligned the project with the company's strategic goals, and identified the key decision makers. Now Jan needs to write the business case.

Everyone on your project team should be involved in the development of your business case. This ensures a broad range of perspectives, and may generate information and ideas that you might have otherwise ignored. However, this does not mean that everyone on the team will write a section of the business case.

Three people are involved on Jan's team: Lisa, Ruth, and Rob. Jan needs to decide which of them should be involved in writing the business-case document.

Lisa

Lisa is the IT expert on the project team. Her input at the research stage of the project has been crucial to the successful analysis of the project's costs, benefits, assumptions, and constraints.

Ruth

Ruth is the marketing expert on the team. She has contributed to the identification of the key decision makers and the questions they are likely to ask.

Rob

Rob is the sales specialist on the team. His knowledge of the company's strategy enabled the team to align the project strategically.

Only one or two people should actually write the business case. However, the content of the business case is usually the result of a team effort.

The business-case writers should be members of the project team. They should have an overall understanding of the project, and be able to synthesize all the team's contributions into one document. Keeping the number of writers to a minimum ensures a consistent style throughout the document.

A business case should not contain excessively technical language or jargon that may not be understood by the audience. You should bear this consideration in mind when you choose a writer. If a member of your team has prior writing experience, this may be a useful skill for writing the business case.

Finally, your chosen writer or writers should have enough time to devote to writing the business case. It's not a good idea to choose someone with restricted availability, regardless of their suitability for the writing task.

Jan meets Lisa, Ruth, and Rob to discuss the designation of the business-case writers.

Jan: Now that we're ready to write the business-case document, we need to designate at most two writers to do the job. Does anyone have any thoughts on who we should choose?

Lisa: Well, my view of things is restricted to the IT area. I wouldn't know that much about the marketing or sales areas, for example. So I don't think I'm the best person to write the business case.

Jan: OK. But obviously your research is going to form a significant part of the case. The same goes for everyone on the team. We need someone who's able to pull the different areas together.

Rob: I could try, but I don't really have much experience in report writing. I think you should be one of the writers, Jan. You're the one with the most comprehensive overview of the whole project.

Jan: OK, I'm happy to take that on. Ruth, I know that you view this project from a marketing perspective. But you have some report-writing experience, right?

Ruth: That's right. I've written a lot of reports that brought together different types of data from just about every source you could think of. It's part of my job.

Jan: Great, that's just what we need. If you'd agree to write the business case with me, then we can get started right away.

Ruth: Sure, I'd be happy to do that.

On the basis of her discussion with her team, Jan decides that she and Ruth should write the business case. As the project leader, Jan has the most comprehensive overview of the project, as well as the most active communication channels with other team members.

Ruth has experience in putting together marketing reports using disparate sources, so her skills will be useful in synthesizing the team members' varied contributions into a single document.

Case Study: Question 1 of 3

Scenario

For your convenience, the case study is repeated with each question.

Ted, a project manager with a large university, is working on a business case for the deployment of a middleware tier in the university's IT network. Now that his team has done the research, Ted needs to decide who should be involved in writing the business case.

Use the Learning Aid Ted's Project Team to get some background on the people involved in Ted's project and determine who should write the business case.

Questions may be answered in any order.

Question

Whose contributions should make it into the final business case?

Options:

1. Just Ted's, as he is the project leader
2. Jack's and Louise's, but not Nathan's as his area of interest is too narrow
3. Everyone on the project team

Answer

Option 1: This is an incorrect option. Ted's job is to coordinate everyone's contribution, including his own, into the business case.

Option 2: This is an incorrect option. Nathan's input is significant and should be included in the business case even if its focus is narrow.

Option 3: This is a correct option. Everyone on the project team should contribute to the development of the business case. However, not everyone should write the actual business case.

Case Study: Question 2 of 3

Which of these considerations should influence Ted in deciding who will write the business case?

Options:

1. Louise's frequent travel abroad means she will not be available to write the business case
2. Nathan's sales knowledge means he should be involved in writing the business case
3. Ted himself should not write the business case, as he does not have enough of an overview of the case
4. Jack's technical nature could be a drawback if he alone writes the business case

Answer

Option 1: This is a correct option. Writing a business case takes time, and Louise's traveling schedule makes it difficult for her to write the business case.

Option 2: This is an incorrect option. As Nathan is not a member of the project team, he is not the best person to write the business case.

Option 3: This is an incorrect option. As Ted is the project team leader, he has the most comprehensive overview of the project.

Option 4: This is a correct option. Jack may assume that the audience is technically literate, and may use over-technical terms.

Case Study: Question 3 of 3

Who should write the business case?

Options:

1. Ted and Jack
2. Ted, by himself
3. Jack, by himself

Answer

Option 1: This is a correct option. Both Ted and Jack have an understanding of the entire project, and Ted has prior experience in writing business cases.

Option 2: This is an incorrect option. Ted has little knowledge of middleware technology, so he would benefit from Jack's input during writing.

Option 3: This is an incorrect option. Jack knows all about the technology, but needs help in writing a case that will be understood by a non-technical audience.

DOCUMENT-DESIGN PRINCIPLES

Document-design principles

The layout and design of your business-case document can help you get your case approved.

Valid research and good writing are essential components of an effective business case. However, creating a document that is easy to read and professional looking can help to ensure that your business case is read.

A well-presented business case has a better chance of succeeding. It impresses the decision makers and demonstrates your team's professionalism.

A well-presented business case can help you avoid some common pitfalls, such as:

insufficient focus

Some business cases contain generic content that fails to focus on the specific business problem and solution. If your business case fails to offer a compelling value proposition, it will be rejected.

lack of structure

Too often, business cases are used as "information dumps," with no persuasive structure or order to the content. This makes it difficult for the reader to find the relevant information.

lack of impact

If the key points of a business case are buried beneath verbosity or jargon, with no visual or cognitive cues to interest the reader, the business case may not be fully read or understood.

poor spelling and grammar

A business case is instantly discredited by such "credibility killers" as misspellings and random capitalization, grammar and punctuation errors, and inconsistent formatting.

Amanda, a senior executive in the Imagenie software company, has just read a business case proposing a new middleware installation. She is unimpressed with the case as it was presented to her.

Insufficient focus

"The proposal didn't appear to meet any of our current business needs. I just couldn't see how middleware would add value to the company's operation at this time."

Lack of structure

"There was a lot of information in the business case, but it didn't seem to be very organized or coherent. For example, I found it hard to see the relevance of a lot of the technical information."

Lack of impact

"I tried to identify the main points of the case, but it was difficult. If it had been a little shorter and a little more clearly written, I might have had some hope."

Poor spelling and grammar

"I spotted several punctuation and spelling errors in the document. It even spelled 'middleware' incorrectly! Frankly, it didn't inspire a lot of confidence."

Amanda, like many corporate decision makers, requires certain things from a business case. She needs to be able to read it easily, to identify the relevant information quickly, and to have confidence in the authority of the business case. Good layout and design can ensure legibility, coherence, and authoritative communication of the most important information where it counts.

When laying out the pages of your business case, you should ensure that there is sufficient white space on your pages - both in line spacing and page margins. It's best to use single-line spacing within paragraphs, and double-line spacing between paragraphs and before headings.

You should leave a margin of one and one-quarter inches on the left-hand side of the page, to allow for binding. The margins on all other sides of the page should be one inch wide, to provide a frame for the content.

You should use the following elements to help make the text on each page more legible:

paragraphs

Paragraphs should be as short as possible for legibility. Paragraphs should deal with only one main point.

formatting

You should use a special format for headings, to set each topic and section apart. Use boldface, underlining, increased font size, or a combination of all of these.

bullet points

Where possible, you should use bullet points to present information concisely. This eliminates the need to use full sentences, thus saving space.

It's important to choose an easy-to-read, business-like typeface for your business case. Document- design experts recommend using serif for text and serif or sans-serif for headings.

Research suggests that serif typefaces are more legible than sans-serif for large blocks of text, whereas sans-serif typefaces are more suitable for headings. The point size of your typeface is also important. You should choose 10-point or 11-point type for all body copy, and 12-point or 14-point type for section headings and subheadings.

If your typeface is smaller than 10 points, your document may be difficult to read. Sam, a regional manager for a clothing retail company, is writing a business case for the creation of a new records-management system. He has created a draft of the business case to show how he wants the document to be laid out.

Sam has incorporated plenty of white space in the margins and between headings and text. He has used consistent formatting, using different styles for main headings and subheadings. His punctuation and spelling are correct. He could improve readability by breaking up the "Solution description" and "Cost and benefit analysis" paragraphs into shorter ones. He could also use bullet lists to break up the text where possible.

You should bind your business case in a durable, high-quality cover. For the most professional-looking result, you should choose a black, blue, or burgundy cover.

The front cover should display:

- the name of the business case,
- the date,
- optionally, the authors of the business case.

Case Study: Question 1 of 3

Scenario

Marsha is writing a business case for the initiation of a usability drive in her organization. She asks you to take a look at the layout she is proposing to use in her business case.

Use the Learning Aid Layout for Marsha's Business Case to determine whether Marsha's business case conforms to good design and layout principles.

Questions may be answered in any order.

Question

Which of these can be said of Marsha's business case?

Options:

1. The key information of the business case stands out
2. It contains persuasive information about the potential value of a usability drive
3. Spelling and capitalization are consistent
4. It does not use jargon or technical terms

Answer:

Option 1: This is an incorrect option. Because Marsha's business case does not contain a problem statement, it is unclear what the core value proposal is.

Option 2: This is a correct option. Marsha's business case offers persuasive information about the value of usability in general. However, it fails to focus on the specific business problem and solution.

Option 3: This is an incorrect option. Marsha's use of capitalization in listing the business case's deliverables is erratic and potentially confusing.

Option 4: This is a correct option. Marsha's case is written in plain English, and can be easily understood by readers who may be unfamiliar with usability.

Case Study: Question 2 of 3

Which of these layout rules does Marsha observe in her business case design?

Options:

1. Include sufficient white space
2. Keep paragraphs as short as possible for legibility
3. Use bullet points
4. Use a suitable typeface for the body of the document

Answer

Option 1: This is a correct option. Marsha's document contains wide margins and sufficient line spacing between paragraphs.

Option 2: This is an incorrect option. Marsha's paragraphs are too long and therefore difficult to read.

Option 3: This is a correct option. The business case has one bullet list. However, there is some content that should be in bullet points, but is not.

Option 4: This is an incorrect option. The business case uses a sans-serif typeface, which should be used only for headings.

Case Study: Question 3 of 3

How could Marsha improve the legibility of her business case?

Options:

1. By making the margins smaller
2. By using more bullet points
3. By formatting heading styles so they are consistent and correspond to the information hierarchy
4. By binding the business case
5. By changing the typeface

Answer:

Option 1: This is an incorrect option. Reducing the amount of white space in the document can make the text more difficult to read.

Option 2: This is a correct option. For example, the information under the "Costs" and "Project description" headings would be clearer if arranged in bullet points.

Option 3: This is a correct option. For example, the subheadings under "Deliverables" should be consistent and in a smaller size than the main headings.

Option 4: This is an incorrect option. Binding the business case does not improve legibility, although it does make the case look more professional.

Option 5: This is a correct option. Using a serif typeface for the main text of the business case may improve legibility.

x

CHAPTER 3 - PRESENTING YOUR CASE

CHAPTER 3 - Presenting Your Case

SECTION 1 - PREPARING THE PRESENTATION

SECTION 1 - Preparing the Presentation

By being well prepared, you avoid many of the pitfalls associated with delivering a business case presentation and greatly increase the chances of your case being heard, and ultimately well received.

Every audience has its own personality. Once you know the makeup of your audience members, you can tailor your message to keep them interested and involved.

Successful presentations do not just happen; they require careful planning, sufficient preparation, and effective delivery methods. Experienced presenters know that certain key elements must be present for their presentations to achieve their objectives and meet their audience's needs.

A well-organized structure will help your audience to follow what you are saying, and when they can follow your argument, they are more likely to come to the same conclusion as you, or agree with your idea.

Creative thinking is a process that can be learned. Using techniques that foster an environment conducive to creative thinking is extremely useful when developing presentations. In this topic, you explored three strategies for idea generation: brainstorming, mind mapping, and affinity diagrams.

Because audiences retain more when they can see as well as hear information, presenters can make use of presentation aids to communicate more effectively. But presentation aids can also be confusing and distracting, and some are expensive, difficult to prepare, and difficult to use. It's important to make sure they achieve a specific purpose and are simple, relevant, and clear.

A WELL-PREPARED BUSINESS CASE PRESENTATION

A well-prepared business case presentation

Preparing an informative, motivational, and persuasive business case is not easy to do.

Well-prepared presentations have an outline that follows logically from point to point. They include supporting statements or evidence for their main points so that listeners can easily follow the rationale of the business case being made. In this lesson, you will learn to think carefully about what you want your presentation to achieve, and develop a realistic series of actions for reaching your objectives.

The decision makers among your audience will be well accustomed to hearing presentations and, as such, will easily distinguish between the well-prepared and the hastily put together presentation.

A well-prepared business case presentation ensures that you:

- develop your content in a logical flow,
- adequately cover your presentation's key points,

- verify that the presentation meets all of its objectives,
- know the needs of your audience.

Question

Ryan is the founding member of the board of directors of a highly successful online travel agency.

He wants to present a business case to his shareholders to promote his ideas for immediate expansion.

How will Ryan benefit from being well prepared before presenting his case?

Options:

1. He will ensure that all his key points are covered
2. He will eliminate the need for flip charts or overhead projectors
3. He will develop his content in a logical flow
4. He will check that the presentation meets all its objectives
5. He will know the needs of his audience
6. He won't need to worry about an introduction

Answer

Option 1: This option is correct. A well-prepared business case will alert him to any of the important points that he may have overlooked.

Option 2: This option is incorrect. Even if a business case is well prepared, visual aids might still be needed to enhance the delivery of information.

Option 3: This option is correct. The best opportunity to order the structure of the content is during the preparation stage. It is then that you will get the best overview of the material and decide on the sequence of content.

Option 4: This option is correct. It is during the preparation stage that the objectives will become clear, and so it is an ideal opportunity to see that they are being addressed.

Option 5: This option is correct. Once he knows his audience, he will be better able to communicate his message to them.

Option 6: This option is incorrect. A good introduction is still a vital part of any well-prepared business case presentation.

ANALYZING AN AUDIENCE

Analyzing an audience

When presenting a business case, the more you understand about how your audience will react to your presentation, the better prepared you will be to tailor the presentation to suit the audience's needs.

Presenters might have charisma or be leading experts in their field, yet their presentations can still fall flat with their audience.

You can develop a presentation that is tailored to your audience's needs by addressing the following four areas:

- size of your audience,
- positions held,
- levels of expertise,
- potentially sensitive issues.

The size of your audience will affect how you interact with it.

Fewer than 30 people

This is a relatively small group and allows you to have eye contact and individual contact with everyone in the room. You can be quite informal in groups of this size.

Between 30 and 50 people

For groups of this size, you have less of a chance for contact with every individual. It may be appropriate to break the audience into smaller groups for some activities.

Over 50 people

Groups of this size allow for the least amount of flexibility. You'll need to make eye contact with different parts of the room, rather than with each individual. You'll probably need a microphone to be heard; use a cordless microphone so you can move around the room.

When analyzing your audience, you need to consider the positions of the people attending the presentation. People at different skill levels in a company prefer to receive information in different ways. These skill levels groups include:

immediate work group

Use "we" language when speaking to members of your own team. Be sure to share success with the entire group. You can be more informal in your tone and use lots of examples and demonstrations to make your point.

upper management

Usually, general management likes to get straight to the bottom line. Streamline your remarks, but back up everything you say with facts. Offer your opinions as suggestions, rather than insisting on them or on particular books of action. Your tone should be a bit more formal.

special interest group

This group requires the most tailoring. Be sure to focus your presentation around the members' particular interests. This may require some extra research and interviewing as you develop your presentation.

mixed group

With a mixed group, you want to include something that appeals to everyone. Make sure you capture the interest of each group in the first few minutes of your presentation.

The level of expertise in your audience influences what you say and how you say it. Even when the group members have little background or experience related to the topic, never talk down to them.

Uninformed

When speaking to uninformed people, be sure to avoid any jargon or acronyms that may be confusing, and don't overwhelm them with too much information.

Informed

With expert technical people, you can assume a level of familiarity with the topic. Suggest rather than instruct, and be sure to involve them in your presentation by asking questions or soliciting questions from audience members.

Another important, but more difficult, aspect of analyzing your audience members is determining whether they have any "sensitive issues." This can make the difference between whether the group is receptive or hostile to your message.

Historical background

Are there any hidden agendas related to the topic? Ask about any incidents that have occurred in the past that may affect the audience's feelings toward the topic.

Resource issues

Determine the resources needed to achieve the objectives in your presentation. Are there different groups competing for the same limited resources? This issue could be a sensitive one with the audience.

Internal conflicts

Assess the personalities involved in the issue, and decide whether they will clash or collaborate. Current conflicts often lead to sensitive issues in an audience.

Current trends

The audience members may be particularly sensitive to certain trends or conditions in their industry or profession.

The better you understand these issues, the more successful your presentation will be. It can change the content, duration, and tone of your entire speech. Different circumstances will call for different styles of presentation.

Question

Select the questions that you should ask about your audience when analyzing it.

Options:

1. What is the size of the audience?
2. What are the levels of expertise in the audience?
3. What is the occupational profile of the audience?
4. How many presentations does the audience attend annually? 5. Are there any sensitive issues concerning the audience?

Answer:

Option 1: That's correct. How you interact with the audience will depend on whether the number of people is small, medium, or large.

Option 2: That's correct. This will inform the degree to which you can employ the use of jargon in your presentation.

Option 3: That's correct. People at different skill levels in a company prefer to receive information in different ways.

Option 4: That's incorrect. This would not be a particularly useful question to ask.

Option 5: That's correct. There may be some particularly divisive issues among your audience that you would want to avoid.

George is a manager at Blue Bay Software. He is preparing to give a presentation on the necessity of an upgrade to the company web site, a potentially costly undertaking. When preparing his presentation, he talks to Bob, a senior manager who has many years of presenting experience.

George: I'm just thinking about the web site presentation that I'll be making next week. It helps that I know who my audience is.

Bob: That's right. You'll be talking to your colleagues. You already have a very good idea of their interests and levels of knowledge. You should use that to your advantage and apply familiar examples and demonstrations when making your point.

George: Yes, knowing that the audience will be experienced and well informed makes it easier for me to tailor my presentation accordingly.

Bob: Right. It's a good idea to present your ideas as suggestions rather than directions, while involving the audience as much as possible in the presentation.

George: People won't be shy about saying exactly what's on their mind. I'd better make sure that I'm very well informed so that I can be prepared for any difficult questions.

Clifford is a senior director at Cargoflow, a shipping and freighting company. He is preparing a presentation to shareholders that proposes relocating their premises closer to the new highway.

While preparing for his presentation, Clifford analyzes his audience and discovers that:

the presentation will be attended by between 30 and 50 people

There will be less of a chance of contact with every individual. Clifford may need to break the audience into smaller groups for some activities.

the audience will be made up of a mixed group of people

The presentation should include something that appeals to everyone. It should try to capture the interests of each group in the first few minutes of the presentation.

they will not be well informed

He should avoid jargon or acronyms that may be confusing, and not overwhelm his audience with too much information.

historically, the shareholders have had a bad experience with a previously unsuccessful attempt to relocate

This is a sensitive issue that the presenter will need to be aware of. Clifford needs to learn about any incidents that have occurred in the past that may affect the audience's feelings toward relocation.

Ruth is one of the founders of the Sherrington chain of hotels. She wants to make a presentation to regional hotel managers that introduces some significant changes to the company's HR policy. While preparing for her presentation, she talks to Ken, a senior director, and asks for some advice.

Ruth: I've been thinking about the presentation that I'll be making about the new HR policies. I'm expecting between 50 and 60 people to attend.

Ken: That's quite a large crowd. You might want to think about using a microphone and a PA system.

Ruth: Yes, that's a good idea. I won't be speaking to any of the audience members on a one-to-one basis during the presentation, so a microphone would work well.

Ken: Given that the audience will comprise mainly of senior management, you shouldn't beat about the bush. Make your point, but back up everything with facts. Try to present your opinions as suggestions rather than recommendations; managers don't like to be told what to do.

Ruth: I've noticed that our new HR policy isn't very popular with a number of managers.

Ken: So I've heard. This is something of a sensitive issue. The main thing is to try to modify your approach somewhat so that you don't exacerbate the situation any further.

Case Study: Question 1 of 4

Scenario

Grace is a financial analyst in a software company that recently experienced a downturn in sales. She is going to present to ten members of the sales team a new, complex accounting system designed to monitor expenses more closely.

There has been considerable disagreement among the sales team about the introduction of this software. Some see it as an efficient way to log expenses, while others regard it as an extra administrative task that they could do without.

She wants to tailor her message to meet the needs of her audience.

Help Grace to analyze her audience by answering the following questions.

Question

Should Grace aim her presentation at an audience that is informed or uninformed?

Options:

1. Informed
2. Uninformed

Answer:

Option 1: That's incorrect. The group comprises salespeople who do not have a background in accounting.

Option 2: That's correct. The group comprises salespeople who do not have a background in accounting.

Case Study: Question 2 of 4

Next, Grace needs to look at the size of her audience and base her presentation style accordingly.

What degree of interaction can Grace expect to have with her audience?

Options:

1. She may need to break the audience into smaller groups for some activities
2. She'll be able to have individual contact with everyone in the room and maintain eye contact
3. She'll probably need a microphone to be heard around the room

Answer:

Option 1: That's incorrect. With a group as small as ten, it would not be necessary to divide it into smaller groups.

Option 2: That's correct. With a small group, she will be able to engage her audience at the individual level.

Option 3: That's incorrect. With a small group, a microphone wouldn't be necessary.

Case Study: Question 3 of 4

What should Grace consider to be of a potential sensitive nature when addressing the audience?

Options:

1. Resource issues
2. Historical background
3. Internal conflicts
4. Current trends

Answer:

Option 1: That's incorrect. Financial resources are not of much importance in this case. If anything, the accounting software should save the company money.

Option 2: That's incorrect. There is no historical issue in relation to the new accounting software.

Option 3: That's correct. There is disagreement within the sales team about the potential inconvenience of the accounting software.

Option 4: That's incorrect. There is nothing about current trends in the business that would create a potentially sensitive issue in this case.

Case Study: Question 4 of 4

Grace will also want to take into account the occupational profile of the group she is about to address.

How should Grace address her audience?

Options:

1. Be more informal and use "we" language when speaking to the audience

2. Focus her presentation around the audience's specific needs

3. Broaden her content to suit a wide range of listeners

4. Streamline her remarks and get straight to the bottom line

Answer:

Option 1: That's incorrect. Grace is from a different department and works in another occupation than that of her audience.

Option 2: That's correct. The sales team will need support taking on the task of learning a new accounting system.

Option 3: That's incorrect. Her audience is quite specific - a sales team - rather than a mixed group.

Option 4: That's incorrect. This approach would be more suitable when addressing senior management.

ELEMENTS OF A WELL-PLANNED PRESENTATION

Elements of a well-planned presentation

We all have certain characteristics, skills, and abilities that make it easier to do certain things. But even when tasks don't come easily, we all have certain characteristics that make it possible for us to learn.

You might feel that you have characteristics that make you a natural presenter. Or you might feel that making presentations is especially difficult for you. Nevertheless, it's useful to identify the characteristics you possess that can help you as a presenter, and to identify the skills and abilities you need to develop.

During a presentation, procedures that you are ordinarily comfortable and familiar with can become difficult due to the distraction or nervousness caused by speaking in front of an audience.

Most attendees travel long and far, sit in several consecutive sessions, and experience information overload. Therefore, the effective presentation should be creative and lively, with a format refreshingly different from the traditional lecture with visual aids.

The presenter should carefully decide on the most audience-friendly, useful way to deliver noteworthy information and help the audience retain it. Good presenters all share some common characteristics.

Good timing

Practice your presentation to ensure that it fits within the time allotted. Tell the audience when questions are permitted. Avoid getting hung up on one slide for too long and then having to fly through the remaining ones too quickly.

Regular eye contact

An effective presenter maintains eye contact with the audience. You should try to look at and speak to your audience, and not the presentation aid that you are using.

Articulate

Good presenters speak clearly and audibly. Mumbling and straying off topic are indicators of inexperience or self-doubt. Assume a professional or casual tone as appropriate to the audience. Better to be too professional than casual.

Professional appearance

The best presenters always dress for success. Avoid overdressing because this can be inappropriate and create a negative impression. Also, avoid excessive body movement or annoying mannerisms. Stand up straight and make the content of your presentation the center of focus.

In order to improve your own presentation skills, you could seek additional training within your own organization. Check with the Training department, the

Education department, or the Human Resources department.

Consider taking classes at a third-level college or university. You can also learn by watching and evaluating presenters you see on television or in seminars or workshops you attend.

Question

Identify the characteristics of effective presenters.

Options:

1. Good eye contact
2. Professional appearance
3. Fast talking
4. Articulate
5. Good use of timing

Answer:

Option 1: This option is correct. Good eye contact will help to communicate your message clearly, and hold your audience's attention.

Option 2: This option is correct. A professional appearance will ensure that you don't offend anyone. It's always better to dress conservatively.

Option 3: This option is incorrect. You should not need to talk quickly. It is more likely that you will be misunderstood if you talk too fast.

Option 4: This option is correct. Good presenters speak clearly and audibly. Mumbling and straying off topic are indicators of incompetence or self-doubt.

Option 5: This option is correct. Good timing is achieved by practicing your presentation and will help to hold the audience's attention.

For any project to be a success, you need planning and preparation. Planning is the process of thinking carefully about what you want to achieve, and developing a realistic series of actions for reaching your objectives. Begin by asking yourself why you are giving the presentation. The answer to this question will be crucial in helping you plan the content.

It's worth taking some deliberate steps to ensure that your presentation is as well planned as possible:

develop objectives

Clearly developed objectives are like the destination on a map. Knowing where you are going is the first step to figuring out the best route.

state the benefits

In persuasive presentations, you need to specifically state the benefits that the audience will receive. Benefits can be stated before the main body of the presentation, or at the end, or ideally in both places.

identify where to use presentation aids

Decide what visual aids or handouts, if any, you want to use with your presentation and where you want to use them. Think about how visual aids can be used to illustrate your major points and sub-points.

develop the conclusion

Good conclusions always return to material in the introduction. Sometimes speakers use a statement that tells the audience what specific actions to take, and when and how to take them.

Question

Anna is due to give a presentation on remote computer access in the workplace. Identify the aspects of a well-planned presentation.

Options:

1. Correct use of visual aids and handouts

2. A developed conclusion
3. Clear objectives
4. Humorous
5. Clearly stated benefits
6. A break in the middle

Answer:

Option 1: That's correct. Think about how visual aids can be used to illustrate your major points and sub-points.

Option 2: That's correct. Use a statement that tells the audience what specific actions to take, and when and how to take them.

Option 3: That's correct. Outline the objectives in advance, paying particular attention to whether the presentation is informative or persuasive.

Option 4: That's incorrect. A well-planned presentation does not have to be particularly humorous.

Option 5: That's correct. It is very helpful for the audience to know about the benefits of a presentation at the beginning.

Option 6: That's incorrect. Unless they are of a particularly lengthy duration, presentations don't necessarily need to have a break in the middle.

David is the production manager for a large software manufacturer. He is planning to give a presentation on the upgrading of the company's online database. He talks to Paul, a senior manager, about how he plans to give the presentation.

David: I've been thinking about the presentation on the new database that I'll be giving next week. I'm trying to think of how I can best illustrate some of the new features of the updated system.

Paul: Well, it would be a good idea to show some screen shots of the new layout. That would be an excellent introduction.

David: For that I should use a PC linked to an overhead projector. Then everyone in the room could have a clear view of the new screen layout.

Paul: You should also think about what the main points of your presentation will be. Break it down into objectives so that you will have a clear picture of what you're including in the presentation.

David: Yes, I was thinking about starting with a visual introduction and then talking people through some of the more important new features. I could finish up with some practical demonstrations using the overhead projector linked to the PC.

Paul: Yes, it's a good idea to have your objectives set out well in advance.

When planning his presentation, David anticipated that he would need to use a presentation aid, in this case an overhead projector linked to a PC. This means he'll have time to source the right equipment well in advance of the presentation, and get a chance to practice using it beforehand.

He also developed his objectives in advance of the presentation. This gave him a clear overview of his presentation content and a strong sense of how he would end the presentation. Used effectively, presentation aids liven up a presentation, hold people's attention, and illustrate concepts in a way that words alone seldom do.

During the planning process, try to identify where presentation aids can help you communicate more effectively and hold audiences' interest. Although you might not be ready to decide exactly which presentation aids to use, you can still identify concepts, facts, or ideas that could be communicated more effectively through the use of some type of presentation aid.

Follow along as David and Paul continue to talk about how to plan for the presentation.

Paul: It's a good idea to let the people know how they can gain from the information you're telling them.

David: Yes, I should let them know what's in it for them. I was planning on telling the audience about how much time will be saved by using this new database. I also want to explain some of the other benefits such as ease of use, efficiency, and improved functionality.

Paul: That's a good idea. How do you think you'll end the presentation?

David: I'm going to briefly go over the main points, particularly what I outlined in the introduction. I'll end by letting everyone know when they can expect the new system to be up and running.

A good conclusion will generally return briefly to what was covered in the introduction. It is also an opportunity to outline what the next step will be in relation to the subject under discussion. In the case of David and Paul, they could explain when the upgrade to the system is due to take place should they decide to go ahead with it.

Just as it takes time to plan a successful business expansion, it also takes time to plan a successful presentation. To use your planning time efficiently, work to develop a preparation method that ensures you include all the aspects of a well-prepared presentation.

Question

Identify the elements of a well-planned business case presentation.

Options:

1. Developed objectives
2. Stated benefits
3. More that one presenter
4. A developed conclusion
5. Correct use of visual aids and handouts

Answer:

Option 1: This option is correct. Clearly developed objectives will help to steer the content of the presentation in the right direction and ensure that the most important points are being covered.

Option 2: This option is correct. Stating the benefits is a very good way to gain the audience's attention. It is worth stating the benefits at both the beginning and toward the end of your presentation.

Option 3: This option is incorrect. It is possible, but by no means necessary, to have more than one person presenting a business case at any given time.

Option 4: This option is correct. A well-structured conclusion will usually refer to what was said in the introduction and touch on what will happen next in relation to the content of the presentation.

Option 5: This option is correct. Visual aids can greatly enhance the impact of a presentation. They are most effective when used to illustrate some of the more important points in the presentation.

A STRUCTURED APPROACH TO THE PREPARATION OF A BUSINESS CASE

A structured approach to the preparation of a business case

One of the greatest fears people have about presentations is that they will get confused, leave things out, or repeat themselves. One way to prevent that happening is to have a sound presentation structure.

The structure helps you to move logically from one point to the next, so it is far less likely that you will leave out a whole section or point in your argument. There are benefits from the point of view of your audience too. Most people find it more difficult to follow and remember information when they are listening, rather than reading. In all presentations, you should tell the audience what you are going to tell them, what you need to tell them, and what you just told them.

All good presentations adhere to this basic structure:

introduction and outline

Build your audience's trust and respect by describing your connection with the subject and providing an outline of what you'll be covering. This is your way of telling them what you are going to tell them.

make clear breaks between subjects

An audience does not always realize when you are making a major change in the direction of a presentation. Making clear breaks between subjects helps the learner grasp what you need to tell them more easily.

use a strong ending

The end of your presentation is your final chance to convince your audience of your point of view. Prompt your audience to reach a decision or change an attitude. The end of the presentation has to be strong — and it needs just as much thought and effort in preparing it as the opening. This is how you tell them what you have told them.

Curtis White is a representative from Central-West Bank. He is giving a presentation to school children between the ages of 15 and 16 about setting up a junior savings account. Curtis gives an outline and intro of his presentation.

Curtis: Hi, my name is Curtis White from the Central-West Bank here in Dryden. Today I'll be talking to you about how to set up a junior savings account at the bank. We'll start off by looking at how you can take money in and out of the bank.

I'll also tell you a little about bank statements, and how to read them. Then I'll finish up by telling you a little about terms and conditions, and how you can get started straight away.

The beginning is one of the most important parts of the presentation. If you make a mistake at this point, it can be very difficult to recover.

Curtis opened the presentation by introducing himself and stating his association with the material he would be covering. He then went on to outline what he would be covering over the book of the presentation.

He told them what he was going to tell them. Curtis is continuing with his presentation on opening a junior savings account. He makes an easy transition toward the conclusion.

Curtis: If at any stage you're not happy with our level of service, or anything else about your savings account, you can talk to your customer service representative and they will be glad to help. So, today we looked at how to open a savings account with as little as one dollar, and how to make deposits and withdrawals.

I would like to sum up by saying that it's never too soon to open a savings account, and that the sooner you start, the easier you'll find saving later on in life. Thank you very much for listening to me today. Good luck with your studies, and we look forward to seeing you down at Central-West Bank.

Curtis did a good job of finishing off his presentation. Once he had finished delivering the main body of his presentation, he concluded by repeating the main point — in this case, that it's never too soon to open a savings account. He then thanked the audience and reminded them that he was looking forward to their business.

Case Study: Question 1 of 2

Scenario

For your convenience, the case study is repeated with each question.

Frank is the owner of Hideaway storage facilities. He wants to make a proposal to his staff of 30 that he would like to move their premises closer to the new highway.

He realizes that this may not be a very popular idea with his employees, as it would involve a further commuting distance for most of them, and the new location would not be near to any shops or restaurants.

But Frank cannot relocate without their support and cooperation.

Help Frank to apply a structured approach to his presentation by answering these questions.

Question

What should Frank use as his opening statement in order to apply a structured approach to his presentation?

Options:

1. "Hi, you all know me. I am, of book, Frank Norton and today I want to talk to you about what a lot of you have been concerned about recently, namely, the idea of our possibly moving the premises out to Highway 62."
2. "Nothing stays the same. The world is in a state of flux and therefore we must be prepared for change. Change is what makes life interesting and a change is exactly what we need."
3. "I remember when I started out in the storage business, I thought to myself: So long as people have belongings, people will want to store their belongings."

Answer:

Option 1: This option is correct. Frank introduces himself to the audience and tells them what he is going to say.

Option 2: This option is incorrect. Frank does not introduce himself or the topic to the audience.

Option 3: This option is incorrect. Frank has not structured his opening. He does not introduce himself or tell the audience the purpose of his presentation.

Case Study: Question 2 of 2

Which statement should Frank use to make a clear transition from the conclusion of his presentation to the ending?

Options:

1. "The opportunities out on Highway 62 are too great to ignore. We can take the high road, or we can stay on the low road. It's up to you. Good bye."
2. "We've looked at the idea of introducing subsidized travel expenses and the addition of a fully stocked canteen at our new premises. I'd like you to think about what I've proposed. Thank you very much for your time, and good bye for now."
3. "The new premises would hold twice as much storage space as our current unit. Think about what's in store for us if we simply stay where we are. Good bye."

Answer:

Option 1: This option is incorrect. Frank didn't restate some of the main points of his presentation and ended it too abruptly.

Option 2: This option is correct. Frank reminded his audience of what he had discussed and thanked them for their time before ending his presentation.

Option 3: This option is incorrect. Frank doesn't make any effort to restate his main points and finishes his presentation without thanking his audience.

GENERATING IDEAS

Generating ideas

There are numerous information resources available to help when researching your presentation. The key is to find the ones that will give you accurate and relevant material.

Useful resources include the Internet, libraries and bookshops, professional and industry organizations, surveys and focus groups, and subject matter experts. These resources are used to help generate ideas, but also to support the ideas once they are generated. The first place most people think of is the Internet.

It is a valuable tool; however, you must be sure that the information you collect is trustworthy. In general, chat sessions give you opinions and may contain misinformation, so use them with caution. A reference librarian or knowledgeable bookseller can guide you to many resources, including:

- Books,
- Magazines,
- Newspapers,

- Journals,
- Government publications.

Professional associations and industry organizations are another source of useful information. They often have research departments designed to share information with members, and often produce publications that offer information targeted to specific professions or industries.

Surveys and focus groups are a good way to collect information from a group of people. You can lead the sessions yourself informally, or you can take on someone to conduct a formal survey.

Brainstorming is a good way to get input and ideas on your presentation topic from a variety of people. Brainstorming is a problem-solving technique, where a group of people sit down and discuss ideas and possible solutions.

Brainstorming was developed initially for liberating people from disciplined ways of thinking and was originally used in the advertising industry. It is best used to generate a large number of ideas quickly.

However, following specific guidelines will increase the likelihood that you'll get the number and quality of ideas you're seeking.

Leader

Use a group of six to twelve people, and appoint a leader who defines the problem, issue, or topic and reminds participants of the ground rules.

Ideas

A brainstorming session is a meeting between people from the same or different departments to solve a problem that affects all involved. All ideas, no matter how bizarre or unrealistic, are explored. The evaluation process will come later.

Notes

Write the ideas on a variety of colors and sizes of sticky notes. That way, when you get to the evaluation process, ideas can be sorted and combined easily.

Break

Spend no more than 25 to 35 minutes brainstorming, and then take a break. After the break, begin evaluating the ideas – new ideas can often emerge from this discussion. Always thank the participants for their help and leave the session feeling energized.

Mind mapping is another popular technique for idea generation. A mind map is a multicolored and image-centered radial diagram that represents connections between portions of learned material. It is good for representing word/phrase associations for people who are visual learners.

Mind mapping improves idea retention because the combination of pictures and words adds visual effect. Mind maps display the creative thought process in a dynamic, rather than a static, way. To create a mind map, you:

select the initial word or phrase

Begin with an idea or a word written in the middle of a blank sheet of paper.

list the associated thoughts

Draw a circle around the word or phrase, and then draw lines away from the center circle. As you think of an association with the first word, create a new circle.

create a web

Continue this process until the word/idea associations have generated a web of ideas, all from the core circle and original word or phrase.

assess the results

Five minutes is usually enough time to create a mind map. Look at the results. Think about how your ideas changed from the original phrase and how creative ideas happen.

An affinity diagram is a technique for organizing a large number of separate ideas into a smaller number of related groups. The affinity diagram is frequently used to look for patterns in ideas and to consolidate the categories of ideas so action can be planned. It is best used for representing word/phrase associations visually.

A key feature is that the organizing groups emerge from the technique instead of being determined in advance.

Sticky notes

The first thing to do is to get all your ideas down on sticky notes. Don't organize or evaluate at this point in the process.

Combine thoughts

After recording your ideas, combine similar thoughts by grouping like items together. You'll start to see general categories and patterns of information.

Brainstorming, mind mapping, and affinity diagrams work very well – they will produce lots of ideas. The best presentations are supported by informative, interesting material.

Question

Match ways of generating ideas with their corresponding descriptions.

Options:

A. Mind mapping
B. Brainstorming
C. Affinity diagram

Targets:

1. Make connections between different sources of material
2. Look for patterns in ideas and consolidate categories of ideas
3. Generate a large number of ideas quickly

Answer

Mind mapping is good for representing word/phrase associations for people who are visual learners.

A key feature of affinity diagrams is that the organizing groups emerge from the technique instead of being determined in advance.

Brainstorming was developed initially for liberating people from disciplined ways of thinking. It was originally used in the advertising industry.

PRESENTATION AIDS

Presentation aids

Relevant, appropriate presentation aids can greatly enhance your presentation. But they can also be distracting and confusing. Additionally, the problems that presentation aids can create could ruin an otherwise excellent presentation. Inappropriate presentation aids can bore the audience and lose its attention.

Selected carefully and used in appropriate ways, presentation aids reinforce, clarify, explain, and illustrate your points and concepts. They also add variety to a presentation, helping engage the audience and hold people's attention. Studies show that audiences remember up to 40% more when they are able to see the information as well as hear what is being said.

A presentation aid is anything you use to reinforce, illustrate, clarify, or explain the information in your presentation including:

- visuals projected on a screen, such as slides and overhead transparencies,

- printed flip chart pages, wall charts, banners, and posters,
- blank surfaces on which to write, such as flip chart pages, white boards, chalkboards, and blank overhead transparencies,
- props, including models, prototypes, and product samples.

Presentation aids can often communicate key points or complex concepts far more effectively than words alone.

Overhead projectors

Overhead projectors are at least as easy to prepare as flip chart pages, and you can use them with a group of any size. The disadvantages are that overhead projectors are noisy and need to be checked out ahead of time to be sure they work.

White boards

White boards offer an easy way to record points generated by your audience, highlight key points, explain concepts with key words or graphics, or present instructions for an activity. White boards are excellent for small groups in small rooms where everyone can see what's written on the board; they are not useful in large auditoriums.

Videos

A carefully produced and edited video can make it easier for people to understand certain concepts or see how something is done and add interest to long presentations.

Other presentation aids are available.

Software applications

For example, spreadsheet packages can display data and graphs, allowing the audience to interactively determine if projected figures and outcomes will be altered if results are different to those planned.

Handouts

Handouts let you give people more information than you can cover during the presentation itself. Whether your handouts are limited to a page or two that summarize key points or are elaborate brochures, they need to be relevant and useful. These include copies of key visuals, workbooks, and information packets. Participants can take hard copies of information away with them.

Consider these guidelines when planning to use presentation aids:

time and cost

Some presentation aids, such as blank flip chart pads, are inexpensive and require very little preparation. But workbooks, information packets, slides, videos, and computer-aided presentations can be time consuming and expensive to prepare. Ask yourself whether value added by a presentation aid justifies the time and cost.

recognize potential problems

The risk of problems increases when you use complicated equipment. If a flip chart easel collapses, you can set it up again or tape pages to the wall. But if a slide projector doesn't work, you can't use your slides. The more complicated the equipment, the more difficult it is to operate and the more likely it is to malfunction.

keep it simple

It can be difficult to read more than a few words on a slide or overhead transparency or flip chart page, especially when it goes by quickly. Each visual should express only one point. Words and pictures should be easy to see from the back row.

direct the audience's attention

Some presenters use so many presentation aids that the audience doesn't know whether to look at the presenter, a blank projection screen, a slide, a prop, or a handout. Make sure you know exactly where you want your audience's attention at each moment of your presentation, and then make sure to draw its attention to that place.

A presentation gives people only one chance to grasp, understand, and remember the presenter's points. Because audiences retain more when they can see as well as hear the information, presenters can make effective use of presentation aids to communicate more effectively.

Presentation technology is changing rapidly. Educate yourself so you are prepared to make the most efficient, effective use of presentation aids to communicate your message clearly.

Question

Scott is about to make his first important presentation. His purpose is to introduce a new marketing campaign to a select group of sales managers at Diallonic Insurance.

He has included a number of aids that he hopes will make his presentation particularly dynamic and exciting. Help Scott identify the appropriate use of presentation aids.

Options:

A. Overhead projectors
B. Videos
C. Handouts
D. White boards

Targets:

1. Show a process in action and stimulate discussion

2. Let you give people more information than you can cover during the presentation itself

3. Can be used with a group of any size

4. Present an easy way to record points generated by your audience, highlighting key areas

Answer:

A video can make it easier for people to understand certain concepts or see how something is done.

Handouts include copies of key visuals, workbooks, and information packets. Participants can take hard copies of information away with them.

The disadvantages of overhead projectors are that they are noisy and need to be checked out ahead of time to be sure they work.

White boards are excellent for small groups in small rooms where everyone can see what's written on the board; they are not useful in large auditoriums.

x

SECTION 2 - DELIVERING THE PRESENTATION

SECTION 2 - Delivering the Presentation

Knowing how to deliver an effective business case presentation will dramatically improve both your confidence and ability to communicate within the business environment.

Even experienced presenters are not immune to the nervousness that can accompany a presentation. In this topic, you have learned how to effectively practice and rehearse your presentation to ensure you present in a spontaneous, relaxed, and confident manner. You have also learned effective methods of combating prepresentation anxiety and relaxation strategies that help reduce nervousness. These skills will prove invaluable in preparing for future presentations.

In this topic, you have learned how to select the most appropriate seating arrangements to suit a given business case presentation. You have also learned ways of controlling the environment both before and during a presentation. In this topic, you have learned how to establish rapport at the beginning of your presentation and how to maintain rapport and keep your audience's attention.

In this topic, you learned how to encourage your audience to ask questions after your presentations. You also learned about some methods you can use to deal with any problems that may arise during discussion.

The closing of your presentation can be as important as the opening.When closing a presentation, you need to restate your main point, tell the audience clearly what is going to happen next, call for action from your audience if necessary, and thank the audience for its time and attention.

KNOWING HOW TO DELIVER

Knowing how to deliver

Anyone who is willing to devote the necessary time and attention to the task can reap the benefits of learning to give successful presentations. Knowing how to make an effective presentation will benefit you in a number of ways:

improved ability to communicate ideas and information

The ability to communicate clearly in a wide range of situations is essential for almost any job. Presentations are the most effective and efficient methods for communicating certain kinds of information.

increased opportunities for career advancement

Delivering successful presentations increases your visibility by helping people get to know you and what you can do. The hard work you put into learning presentation skills will help you achieve your career goals.

increased self-confidence

Every new skill increases self-confidence, especially when learning the new skill means challenging yourself to overcome reluctance or fear.

Lee's team leader asked all members of the team to give a presentation about areas they feel need improvement. Lee has just delivered his presentation. He was happy to be given the opportunity to plan his points and present them clearly. He was able to communicate his opinions to the team logically, and did not feel like he was "on the spot" to think of something.

His team leader commented on how well he made the presentation and told him how important it was to be able to communicate his ideas and that it shows management exactly what he is capable of. Lee felt confident that he was able to deliver the presentation successfully and was happy with the praise he received.

Question

Select the benefits of being able to deliver an effective business case presentation.

Options:

1. Increased self-confidence
2. Ability to communicate ideas and information more effectively
3. Increased ability to produce a presentation without the need for planning
4. Increased opportunities for career advancement

Answer:

Option 1: This option is correct. Learning any new skill will inevitably increase your confidence, particularly presenting in front of an audience.

Option 2: This option is correct. As a result of knowing how to deliver a business case effectively, you will improve your overall communication skills.

Option 3: This option is incorrect. You will always need to plan the presentation in advance. The better prepared you are, the better your presentation will be.

Option 4: This option is correct. Making good presentations will increase your profile both within and beyond your organization.

REDUCING STRESS BEFORE GIVING A PRESENTATION

Reducing stress before giving a presentation

You can't make feelings of presentation fear disappear. Even the act of trying to ignore them can make them worse. But you can take some steps to reduce the anxiety you feel before a presentation and to control the nervousness you feel during the presentation itself. It's not only beginners who experience presentation fear. Experienced presenters often find that they feel some tension in the days and weeks before an important presentation.

Even people who feel confident when they walk into the presentation room sometimes discover themselves unexpectedly anxious when they stand up to speak. When presenters are anxious, they may experience nervous and physical tension, a lack of confidence, a lack of focus. They become unable to see themselves making a successful presentation.

Here are some steps you can take to reduce the anxiety you feel before giving a presentation.

Visualize

Visualizing is a form of practicing in which you walk through an activity in your mind, in order to build confidence in your skills. Also known as "imaging," visualization is most helpful after you've practiced delivering the presentation aloud and on your feet. Visualization is not a substitute for practice. It's a good activity to do the night before your presentation, in the privacy of your own home.

Meditate

Meditating helps some people relax and center themselves. You don't need to chant a mantra; just find a quiet, private place, close your eyes, and clear your mind. Some presenters find that meditating the night before a presentation or just before the presentation itself helps them focus and control nervous tension.

Exercise

For some people, the best stress reliever is physical exercise. Some presenters find that they reduce the symptoms of stage fright by working off their tension: going for a brisk walk, going to the gym, or even climbing up and down stairs. While it's important not to exhaust yourself, you might find exercise helpful for relieving physical tension.

Making a presentation can be very stressful. When you're under stress, it's even more important than usual to get enough rest, eat properly, get sufficient exercise, and find ways to relax. Nervousness produces physical symptoms that make it very difficult to deliver a relaxed, confident presentation.

Physical symptoms of nervousness include:

- dry mouth,

- rapid, shallow breathing,
- tense neck and shoulder muscles,
- tense facial muscles and locked jaw,
- shaking hands and legs.

These physical symptoms of nervousness can be controlled using relaxation strategies:

breathe

Presenters often experience rapid, shallow breathing. If you realize that you are not breathing normally, stop talking until you can get your breathing under control. Take a deep breath through your nose, then exhale through your mouth, and hold your breath. Your body, which needs oxygen, takes over and breathes on its own. Repeat the process several times, until you are breathing normally.

release tension as it occurs

Nervousness often manifests itself in shaking hands and legs. If you realize that you are experiencing these symptoms, try to just let them go and relax. Try to become aware of these symptoms as they occur in your everyday life. The more often you practice becoming aware of these symptoms and overcoming them, the quicker you'll be able to overcome them during a presentation.

yawn

Nervous presenters often experience dry mouth, tense facial muscles, and locked jaw. Yawning is a good way to relax jaws and facial muscles, and also increases the amount of saliva in your mouth. Although you don't want to yawn during a presentation, yawing several times is a good way to relax before the presentation starts.

loosen muscles in your head and shoulders

Many presenters experience tense necks and shoulders. Loosening up these muscles before the presentation helps you feel and look more relaxed. Try breathing deeply as you rotate your head up, down and to the left and right. Also try lifting your shoulders up as high as they can go, and then dropping them slowly until they reach their normal position.

Question Set

Julie is a newly recruited car saleswoman and has to make a presentation to potential buyers. Answer these question to help Julie overcome anxiety and nervousness.

Question 1 of 2

Anxiety before a presentation can cause a number of negative symptoms, but these can be easily overcome by taking some simple steps.

Match these symptoms of anxiety with their solutions. Drag the letters on the left to the boxes on the right. Each letter may be used only once.

Options:

A. Lack of confidence and inability to imagine yourself making a successful presentation

B. Experiencing nervous tension and becoming unfocused

C. Stress and physical tension

Targets:

1. Visualize
2. Meditate
3. Exercise

Answer:

Visualizing is a form of practicing in which you walk through an activity in your mind, in order to build confidence in your skills.

Meditating helps some presenters relax and center themselves. Meditating the night before a presentation or just before the presentation itself helps them focus and control nervous tension.

For some people, the best stress reliever is physical exercise. Some presenters find that they reduce the symptoms of stage fright by working off their tension.

Question 2 of 2

Nervousness can cause a number of physical symptoms, but these can be easily controlled using relaxation strategies.

Match these symptoms of nervousness with their solutions. Drag the letters on the left to the boxes on the right. Each letter may be used only once.

Options:

A. Rapid, shallow breathing

B. Unsteady hands and legs

C. Dry mouth, tense facial muscles, and locked jaw

D. Tense neck and shoulder muscles

Targets:

1. Breathe
2. Release tension as it occurs
3. Yawn
4. Loosen muscles in your head and shoulders

Answer

If you realize that you are not breathing normally, stop talking until you can get your breathing under control. Take a deep breath through your nose, then exhale through your mouth, and hold your breath.

If you realize that you are experiencing these symptoms, try to just let them go and relax. Practice doing this in your everyday life.

Yawning is a good way to relax jaws and facial muscles, and also increases the amount of saliva in your mouth.

Loosening up these muscles before the presentation helps you feel and look more relaxed.

x

WAYS TO PRACTICE AND REHEARSE

Ways to practice and rehearse

When presenting a business case, your presentation skills must be impressive and able to withstand the scrutiny of senior managers and directors. Therefore, practicing your presentation is vital. A well-practiced presentation stands out while an underpracticed one is merely average.

To be able to present in a spontaneous, relaxed, and confident manner, you need to be very familiar with your material. The only way to achieve this is with plenty of practice. As you practice your presentation, you will notice you become less hesitant, increase in volume, and develop a confident conversational tone.

You should practice every part of your presentation, including the equipment you intend to use, such as overhead projectors, laptops, microphones, and laser pointers. There are a number of stages in practicing a presentation, which focus on both your vocal and physical presentation skills.

By following these stages you can ensure that you are familiar with your material and you present in a spontaneous, relaxed, and confident manner:

practice aloud

Practicing your presentation aloud helps you identify words and sentences that may sound good on paper, but are difficult to say. Once you have identified these words and sentences you can practice them until you can say them correctly.

audio record your presentation

By recording your presentation with an audio tape recorder, you can identify any vocal issues such as inappropriate tone, wrong pace, or bad grammar in advance. These audio recordings can be reviewed to help you become more familiar with the material.

transcribe your audio recording

Reviewing your transcription helps you to eliminate any unnecessary details and redundant words. Try to keep your presentation clear and concise.

present for peers

Practice your presentation for your peers. They will point out any inappropriate body language, and provide constructive feedback on your material and presentation skills.

video record your presentation

You may also want to video record your presentation and review it to help you identify and eliminate any odd gestures or body language, and give you an overall idea of how you look and sound.

Question

Identify the ways to practice and rehearse before delivering a presentation.

Select all that apply.

Options:

1. Audio record your presentation
2. Practice aloud
3. Present for peers
4. Stay up all night reviewing your script
5. Transcribe your audio recording
6. Video record your presentation
7. Practice using the equipment you intend to use

Answer

Option 1: This option is correct. Audio recording your presentation enables you to identify in advance any vocal issues such as inappropriate tone, wrong pace, or bad grammar.

Option 2: This option is correct. Practicing your presentation aloud helps you identify words and sentences that may sound good on paper, but are difficult to say, and practice saying these words and sentences.

Option 3: This option is correct. Presenting for your peers enables you to get constructive feedback on your material and presentation skills.

Option 4: This option is incorrect. It important that you are well rested on the day of your presentation.

Option 5: This option is correct. Transcribing your audio recording enables you to eliminate any unnecessary details and redundant words and keeps your presentation clear and concise.

Option 6: This option is correct. Video recording your presentation helps you identify and eliminate any odd gestures or body language, and gives you an overall idea of how you look and sound.

Option 7: This option is correct. Practicing using the equipment you intend to use helps eliminate any technical difficulties that may arise on the day.

OPTIMIZING THE ENVIRONMENT

Optimizing the environment

Having the right setting for your presentation is advantageous for both you and your audience. Delivering your presentation in the most suitable conditions will help you and your audience be more comfortable. It will help the presentation to run more smoothly and help the group to focus.

Having an inappropriate setting may cause the audience to become distracted and it will not be able to concentrate on you or the presentation. A room that's too large can make it difficult for an audience to focus. A room that's too small means that the people will feel crowded.

If possible, select a room that is square rather than rectangular and that is just large enough for the size of group you expect and the room setup you plan to use.

Will you want an informal or formal atmosphere? Will people need to talk to one another, take notes, or do activities?

The way you set up the room establishes the relationship of the participants to you and to each other. The room setup can encourage or discourage participation and affect the participants' ability to see and hear easily. The room to be used for the presentation should be optimized so that it meets your needs by considering the:

seating arrangement

Seats should be set out in a way that allows the audience members to look at each other, and allows the presenter to see everyone in the audience easily.

position of equipment used

Equipment has to be positioned so that it is convenient to use. Furthermore, the audience should be allowed to easily focus on the content of the presentation and not be distracted by the mode of presentation. For example, a projector and a projection screen should be positioned so that all the audience have clear view of the presentation.

size and shape of room

The room should be of a size for the number of people in the audience, and of a shape that enables the presenter to communicate with everyone. So, if there is a choice of rooms, the room should be chosen carefully. Temporary partitions are very useful for adjusting the size of a room.

Question

Which aspects of a room setup should you try to optimize before giving a presentation?

Options:

1. Possible distractions
2. Position of equipment
3. Soothing music
4. Size and shape of room

5. Seating arrangement

Answer:

Option 1: This option is correct. There is always the potential for unforeseen distractions such as noisy ventilation or heating and air conditioning systems.

For this reason, distractions should be eliminated if possible.

Option 2: This option is correct. It's important to make sure that the projector and projection screen allow the audience to clearly focus on the content of the presentation.

Option 3: This option is incorrect. The use of music would not be an important consideration when optimizing the presentation environment.

Option 4: This option is correct. The size and shape of the room should suit the number of people in the audience and allow the presenter to communicate clearly with the audience.

Option 5: This option is correct. Seating should be set up in such a way as to allow the presenter to communicate clearly and to maximize the contribution from and interaction among the audience members.

The most suitable seating arrangement for the presentation of a business case depends on the size of the audience and the extent to which audience members need to interact with each other and the presenter.

The possible seating arrangements include:

auditorium

The audience sits in fixed seats or chairs facing the presenter. This works well where there is a large audience, such as that at conferences. This arrangement works well if audience participation or interaction is not essential. A typical auditorium will have a tiered seating arrangement so that the audience members at the back will not feel isolated.

classroom

In this arrangement, the audience members face the presenter and sit in separate, sometimes portable seats, often in rows and columns. This setup encourages interaction with the presenter but discourages interaction among the audience members. This may be suitable for medium-sized audiences that need to take notes.

workgroup

People are arranged around a single table. This encourages interaction but works best for small groups and where the tables of different size can be used, and where the seating is flexible. This option usually gives the audience the opportunity to write and use computers during the presentation.

Question

Match the description of the audience and the interactivity required with the most suitable seating arrangement.

Options:

A. A large audience where audience participation or interaction is not essential

B. A few people who need to interact with each other and with the presenter

C. A group of medium size where interaction with the presenter is important

Targets:

1. The audience sits in fixed positions in rows and columns facing the presenter in a room of average size

2. A small room where the seating arrangement and table size can be varied

3. A huge room with tiered seating in fixed positions

Answer:

Classroom seating discourages interaction among the audience but the relatively large size of the audience may force the presenter to use this arrangement.

Workgroup seating encourages interaction and is very useful for activities such as brainstorming sessions.

Auditoriums are suitable for conference speeches.

Question

Match the description of the audience and the interactivity required with the most suitable seating arrangement.

Options:

A. A large audience where audience participation or interaction is not essential

B. A few people who need to interact with each other and with the presenter

C. A group of medium size where interaction with the presenter is important

Targets:

1. The audience sits in fixed positions in rows and columns facing the presenter in a room of average size

2. A small room where the seating arrangement and table size can be varied

3. A huge room with tiered seating in fixed positions

Answer:

Classroom seating discourages interaction among the audience but the relatively large size of the audience may force the presenter to use this arrangement. Workgroup seating encourages interaction and is very useful for activities such as brainstorming sessions. Auditoriums are suitable for conference speeches.

There are some occasions when, for example, the seating arrangements or size of the venue are beyond your control. However, in planning a presentation, you must still attempt to optimize the environment in which it will be delivered to cater to the size of the audience and the type of interactivity required.

It is important to choose a room that best suits the needs of your presentation. You should then set up the room exactly the way you want it. A poor presentation environment can take away from the content of your actual presentation. The room to be used for the presentation needs to meet requirements in terms of the:

size and shape

The room to be used for the presentation must be large enough to accommodate all the audience, but small enough to maximize the interaction between the audience and with the presenter. This often makes choosing a room the initial consideration.

position of equipment

It is essential that both the presenter and audience can easily focus on the content of the presentation. So, if using a projector, it should be positioned so that it is easy for the presenter to use but it should also not block the view of any of the audience. And the audience should have a clear view of the projection screen without having to, for example, face in a different direction to that which they use when taking notes.

seating

Seats should be arranged in a way that it is appropriate for the type of activity required. Flexible seating encourages the audience members to exchange ideas but if interaction between audience and presenter is the only type of discussion required, then one-person seats in fixed positions may be acceptable.

Choose your presentation environment carefully and make adjustments to avoid some common problems such as insufficient seating for audience members, uncomfortable seating, noise distractions in the presentation room, poorly positioned flip charts or projectors, and poor heating and ventilation.

The size and shape of the room you use in your presentation can be critical to how successful it can be.

Narrow room

A narrow room may mean that a lot of your audience members have to sit farther away from you. They may have difficulty concentrating on what is being said and shown.

Square room

If possible, use a square room that is just the right size for your group and seating plan.

Room size

A room that's too small can make the audience feel overcrowded and uncomfortable. A room that's too large can make it hard for the audience to focus. Try to get a room that is the perfect size for your group.

The are three main seating arrangements suitable for the presentation of a business case:

auditorium seating

This is ideal for a large audience. People are in fixed seats or chairs facing the presenter. It's almost impossible to take notes or do activities from an auditorium seat.

classroom-style seating

This is where people sit at tables arranged in rows and columns facing the presenter. It gives people space to write or work at computers, but this setup discourages interaction.

conference-table seating

People are arranged around a single table. This encourages interaction but works well only for very small groups. For larger groups, people cannot easily see others on their side of the table.

The type of seating arrangement you use for your presentation depends on when and how you use it.

Auditorium seating

Auditorium seating is used for presentations that involve large groups. The presentation is usually formal. This works well for speeches that require no audience participation or interaction between audience members.

Classroom-style seating

Classroom-style seating is good for a small or medium-sized audience. It is useful for when the presenter can move into the audience easily.

Conference-table seating

Conference-table seating can be used for small or large groups. The presenter must stay in the presentation area. This is particularly constructive for small groups as it offers intimacy for discussion. For large groups, the conference table is useful for computers and note-taking. Conference-table seating is also practical for issuing handouts.

Case Study: Question 1 of 2

Scenario

For your convenience, the case study is repeated with each question. Tricia is preparing a presentation to employees on the role of HR in the company. As part of her preparation, she needs to decide which room she wants and how to optimize the room for the presentation.

Question

Select the most suitable room for Tricia's presentation.

Options:

1. A small room with a large round table in the middle and a VCR and TV screen in the corner
2. A large room with seats positioned to face the presentation area
3. A medium-sized room with a projector positioned at the back wall

Answer:

Option 1: This option is incorrect. A table positioned in the middle of the room would obstruct the line of sight between the projector and the screen.

Option 2: This option is incorrect. In this case the audience needs a surface area to write on in order to complete the questionnaire. A large room can have an isolating effect on smaller groups of people.

Option 3: This option is correct. Tricia needs a medium-sized room with the projector out of the way behind the audience so as not to obstruct its view of the presentation area.

Case Study: Question 2 of 2

Which seating arrangement should Tricia use for the HR presentation?

Options:

1. Seating in columns and rows facing the presentation area
2. Seating at individual desks
3. Seating arranged around a large table

Answer

Option 1: This option is incorrect. There would be no need for a computer at each desk as the questionnaire will be handwritten.

Option 2: This option is correct. The audience will need individual writing areas in order to complete the questionnaire.

Option 3: This option is incorrect. This would not provide any confidentiality for when the participants fill out their questionnaires.

A perfect presentation environment won't do much to help a poorly prepared presentation — but a poor environment can ruin an otherwise excellent presentation. The success of your presentation doesn't just depend on good preparation and rehearsal. You need to control the presentation environment as much as possible.

You might have found that the room was too small and crowded, that the seating arrangement made it hard to see the presenter or the visuals, or that the room was uncomfortably warm or cold.

Other problems could have been that the chairs were uncomfortable, the room was noisy, the lighting was poor, or you didn't have a place to take notes. A presenter can optimize the environment to suit their needs during a presentation by:

asking questions in advance

Find out everything you can about the room, the setup, and other environmental factors ahead of time.

providing a drawing

To avoid misunderstandings, provide the people in charge of the room setup with a detailed drawing that illustrates how the presentation will be conducted. Make sure people understand why the room selection and setup is important.

arriving early

By arriving an hour ahead of time, you can make last-minute adjustments in the setup and become familiar with the room. For example, you can check to make sure everyone can see flip charts or slides and move chairs and tables if they're not in the right configuration.

supplementing poor lighting

Poor lighting not only makes it hard to see, but it induces a negative atmosphere in a room. If necessary, bring in lamps to add more light.

adjusting the content and mode of your presentation if necessary

If you can't make an essential change to the environment, change the presentation if possible. For example, people won't be able to do a lot of writing or engage in small-group discussions if they're tightly packed into auditorium seats.

Alex had to deliver a presentation to his company about its performance in the last quarter. This was Alex's first major presentation and he wanted to prepare well.

He went to the facilities manager to find out more information about the presentation room such as air-conditioning and lighting. He gave the facilities manager a seating layout and marked locations where he would need extra lighting. Alex has scheduled to be free the hour before his presentation so he can arrive early in case any adjustments need to be made.

Question

Select the ways in which a presenter of a business case can improve their environment during a presentation.

Options:

1. Ask questions in advance
2. Supplement poor lighting
3. Arrive early
4. Ensure the temperature is just below room temperature to keep the audience alert
5. Provide a drawing

Answer

Option 1: This option is correct. The more you know about the room in advance, the better able you'll be to tailor your presentation to suit the room.

Option 2: This option is correct. If the room is too dark, you may want to supplement the lighting with more lamps or spotlights.

Option 3: This option is correct. Arriving early will give you the chance to familiarize yourself with the room and make any necessary adjustments.

Option 4: This option is incorrect. It would not be necessary to lower the temperature to keep the audience alert. You should rely on your content to engage the audience.

Option 5: This option is correct. Providing a detailed drawing of how you envisage the environment will help to ensure that you get exactly what you want.

x

MAINTAINING A RAPPORT WITH THE AUDIENCE

Maintaining a rapport with the audience

Successful presenters establish rapport right away and maintain that rapport throughout the presentation. They project the sense of confidence that comes from careful planning and preparation. They know how to reduce and control the symptoms of anxiety and nervousness.

You can begin establishing rapport even before you step up to the podium. Unless you are making a dramatic entrance from behind a curtain, you are "on stage" as soon as people enter the room. Some presenters like to stand at the door and greet people as they arrive.

Others remain in the "presenter's area" at the front of the room but establish nonverbal contact with a nod and a smile as people enter. Still others enjoy mingling with the group as people find their seats and settle down. Whatever methods you prefer, keep in mind that the connection you make with your audience helps people feel comfortable and makes it easier to communicate your message.

Establish rapport by making eye contact with people and perhaps greeting them as they arrive. Begin on time and get the audience's attention before launching the presentation with your carefully prepared opening. Make sure you communicate clearly by watching your volume, pace, tone, diction, and body language. To help the presentation go smoothly, maintain eye contact with your audience throughout the presentation so you can spot cues that people are confused or restless. Keep discussions on track and respond quickly to problems.

You can use three useful techniques when trying to establish and maintain a rapport with your audience while making a business case presentation:

- get the audience's attention,
- provide a road map of the presentation,
- state the benefits of your case.

Gaining the audience's attention is your first challenge.

To do this, you will need to draw the audience in at the beginning of your presentation. You can use an interesting story, a startling statistic, or a quote from a famous person. Listeners will remember ideas or information they heard first during a speech or presentation. When you begin any presentation, you must realize that, to a large extent, the audience members are still engaged in whatever they were doing before they came into the room.

Your job is to get them to shift their attention, and focus on you exclusively. You can draw the attention of your audience in a number of ways:

personal experience

"Last year, I discovered an amazing document in a folder I was about to throw away. That document changed my life..."

hypothetical situation

"How would you feel if you came in to work tomorrow to find that you'd been given a six-month leave, with full pay?"

startling fact

"House prices in this area have risen an average of 25% in the last year."

rhetorical question

"Who here would like to earn more money?"

reference to recent news

"As the president said last week..."

famous quote

"To quote Neil Armstrong, 'That's one small step for man, one giant leap for mankind.'"

Question

Joe is a salesman who has to make a presentation on a new computer gaming console to potential buyers.

How should Joe get the audience's attention?

Options:

1. "When I first played this console I could not believe my eyes."
2. "Our developers spent many long hours in the lab developing this games console."
3. "How would you like to experience driving a formula one racing car, or flying a spacecraft?"
4. "Thank you all for taking the time to come to this presentation."

Answer:

Option 1: This option is correct. Joe is telling the audience of an amazing personal experience, which captures its attention.

Option 2: This option is incorrect. Joe telling the audience about a mundane situation that will not grab its attention.

Option 3: This option is correct. Joe asks the audience a rhetorical question about an interesting situation, which draws its attention.

Option 4: This option is incorrect. Joe is not saying anything that will grab the audience's attention, or encourage it to listen to what he is going to say next.

The road map is the way you orient your audience to the topic and outline what you will talk about. It will also help audience members to focus on your presentation and give them a sense of the direction you are going to take. The basic technique is to give your subject a recognizable beginning, middle, and end.

With the road map, you help the audience to understand the main points of your presentation so it will understand where you are, and how you will arrive at your conclusion. This will give the audience confidence that you are not speaking "off the top of your head."

Follow Brian, a pharmacist who has researched a new cancer-treating drug, as he provides a road map for his presentation by giving his subject a recognizable beginning, middle, and end.

First of all I'll tell you about how I tested the drug and what conclusions I was able to make about it.

Then, I'll compare this drug to similar drugs available today.

Finally, I'll outline the advantages that this drug holds over its competitors.

Question

Brian has captured the audience's attention and is now ready to provide a road map for his presentation. Which statement does this the best?

Options:

1. "Today I'll tell you why this drug is the most scientifically advanced on the market. I'm so sure of this that I guarantee you'll run out and buy one as soon as I'm finished!"
2. "I'll start by outlining the features of the drug, and then show you graphically how it works. Finally, I'll describe why this is the best drug on the market today."
3. "When I'm finished with this presentation, there will be no doubt in your mind that this is the best drug ever made."

Answer

Option 1: This option is incorrect. Joe does not explain how his presentation is going to go, and does not outline a clear beginning, middle, and end to the presentation.

Option 2: This option is correct. Joe is giving his presentation a recognizable beginning, which helps the audience focus on his presentation and gives it a sense of the direction he is going to take.

Option 3: This option is incorrect. Joe does not give the audience a sense of where the presentation is going, or how it can come to this realization.

There are distinct differences between benefits and features. Too often people will talk about features, which may or may not appeal to the audience.

Think about that old saying, "What's in it for me?" This is really what the audience wants to know.

To come up with benefits, think of questions or problems the audience would like answered. For example:

- "How will I get my work finished faster?"
- "How can this make my job easier?"

Explaining true benefits will help to establish a rapport with the audience, and get the maximum results from a presentation.

Follow as Brian states the benefits the audience receives from his findings, in order to establish a rapport with the audience. "The advantages of this drug are that it is more effective, safer, and has fewer and less severe side effects than its competitors."

Question

Which of these statements has the best example of how Brian should tell the audience of the benefits of the new drug?

Options:

1. "This drug is by far the most advanced drug on the market. Patients will never need another one."

2. "The effectiveness of this drug is far superior to any other drug available on the market. It has been developed based on the latest research and uses the latest in scientific technology."

3. "This drug is more effective, safer, and has fewer and less severe side effects than any other drug of its kind currently on the market."

Answer

Option 1: This option is incorrect. Brian does not explicitly explain why it is a benefit to the audience to have "the most advanced drug on the market." This will not help his rapport with the audience.

Option 2: This option is incorrect. Brian is presenting features, not benefits. He can present the features during the presentation. Right now he should be building rapport by presenting benefits.

Option 3: This option is correct. Brian explains the true benefits of the drug, which helps to establish a rapport with the audience, and gets the maximum results from a presentation.

METHODS FOR ESTABLISHING AND MAINTAINING GOOD AUDIENCE RAPPORT

Methods for establishing and maintaining good audience rapport

Jane is a manager with Accounts Now, a highly successful financial services company. She wants to give a presentation to introduce a new accounting software package to the company's team of accountants. She recognizes the importance of establishing and maintaining a rapport with her audience in order for her presentation to be properly effective.

Follow along as Jane gives her presentation. Notice how she tries to establish a rapport with the audience by grabbing its attention from the outset.

"Elvis Presley once said that he didn't have any use for bodyguards, but that he did need two highly trained certified public accountants. As accountants, we are in demand. But we are still in competition. More and more American companies are losing revenue because of their failure to keep their software applications up to date. The last company I worked for thought it could survive without investing in software applications. Within six months, it had to close down, because it could not keep up with the competition."

Jane immediately got the attention of her audience by quoting Elvis Presley and following up by giving an account of a personal experience. This is the first step to take when trying to establish a rapport with your audience.

Get its attention. Follow Jane as she uses different methods to grab the attention of her audience.

"There has never been so many accounting firms in the US all competing for the same business. Last year, 857 new accounting firms entered the industry. The industry is becoming far more competitive, and more and more American companies are losing revenue because of their failure to keep their software applications up to date. Imagine trying to run a competitive accounting firm using old paper-based ledger books. It would be impossible. Technology is constantly moving on and we must keep up in order to remain competitive.

How can a company stay competitive if it does not keep up with the competition?" In this example, Jane uses a different approach to grab her audience's attention.

She starts by giving them a startling fact, followed by a hypothetical situation and a rhetorical question. By using a number of these attention-grabbing strategies, Jane can ensure that her audience is listening to her, and is interested in what she will say next. Having gotten the audience's attention, Jane now wants to continue to maintain a rapport with it. Follow along as she continues her presentation.

"I want to talk to you today about how our accountancy software needs are changing, and how I propose we ensure that our needs are being met. Later I'd like to talk a little about training and specifically about how this package will be available to us on a portable PDA. I'll then finish up by giving you an overview of some of the new features included in the new software."

Jane laid the groundwork for maintaining a rapport with the audience by letting it know what she was going to talk about. This gives the audience confidence in the speaker and reminds it of the relevance of the presentation. In other words, this helps to hold its attention and contributes to the rapport in the presentation. Jane continues with her presentation.

"This software will speed up your processes, cut down on your administration costs, and ultimately make you more competitive in your industry." By letting the audience members know what's in it for them, Jane maintained a rapport by holding their attention.

Question

Identify the methods Jane should use in order to establish and maintain a rapport with the audience.

Select all that apply.

Options:

1. Get its attention
2. Shake hands with every member of the audience
3. Provide a road map
4. Provide drinks and snacks for the audience
5. State the benefits

Answer:

Option 1: This option is correct. Gaining the audience's attention is the first step Jane should take. This can be an interesting story, a startling statistic, or a quote from a famous person.

Option 2: This option is incorrect. It is not necessary to shake hands with every member of the audience. Some presenters like to greet people as they arrive, or establish nonverbal contact with a nod and a smile as people enter.

Option 3: This option is correct. Providing a road map gives your subject a recognizable beginning, middle, and end and ensures the audience that you are not speaking "off the top of your head."

Option 4: This option is incorrect. It is not necessary to provide drinks and snacks for the audience, as this will more than likely distract the audience's attention.

Option 5: This option is correct. Stating the benefits of your case outlines what the audience gets from your presentation.

Case Study: Question 1 of 3

Scenario

For your convenience, the case study is repeated with each question. Mary is a civil servant who has to make a presentation to her managers, proposing a tightening in the drunk driving laws. Help Mary maintain a rapport with the audience by answering the following questions.

Question

Which of these statements should Mary use to get her audience's attention?

Options:

1. "Drunk driving causes 63% of all road accidents."
2. "In this presentation I will address the impact of alcohol on the driver. I will then outline my recommendations and finally I will describe the effects of implementing my recommendations."

3. "The benefit of tightening the drunk driving laws will be a reduction in the number of people killed on our roads."

Answer:

Option 1: This option is correct. Mary grabs the attention of the audience by giving it a startling fact.

Option 2: This option is incorrect. Mary does not draw the attention of the audience. Instead, she gives it a road map of her presentation.

Option 3: This option is incorrect. Mary outlines the benefits of her presentation, but she does not get the audience's attention by opening with this.

Case Study: Question 2 of 3

How does Mary effectively provide a road map of her presentation?

Options:

1. "We are all here today to find out why we need to tighten our drunk driving laws. It is important that we all know the impact of drunk driving and the effects that just one alcoholic drink can have on someone's driving ability."

2. "I hope that by the end of this morning's presentation you will all know why we need to tighten this country's drunk driving laws. We need to do this in order to reduce the number of people killed on our roads."

3. "In this morning's presentation I will outline the extent of damage that alcohol has on a driver. I will then outline my recommendations and finally I will describe the effects of implementing my recommendations."

Answer:

Option 1: This option is incorrect. Mary does not give any idea as to how she is going to structure her presentation and just gives the audience general information about the content of her presentation.

Option 2: This option is incorrect. Here, Mary tells the audience the reason for the presentation, but she does not tell it how she is going to present this information.

Option 3: This option is correct. Mary gives the audience a road map for the presentation, by defining a start, middle, and end to the presentation.

Case Study: Question 3 of 3

Identify ways that Mary can state the benefits of tightening drunk driving laws.

Options:

1. "Do you know what sort of impact one glass of wine has on your driving skills?"
2. "Every citizen can benefit if drunk driving laws are tightened."
3. "The benefit of tightening the drunk driving laws is saving the lives of our citizens."

Answer:

Option 1: This option is incorrect. Asking the audience a question is a way of getting its attention. However, it does not indicate the benefit of tightening drunk driving laws.

Option 2: This option is incorrect. Mary does not state the benefit of tightening drunk driving laws.

Option 3: This option is correct. Mary outlines the benefits of her proposal with this statement.

MANAGING QUESTIONS AND ANSWERS

Managing questions and answers

By including a question and answer session in your presentation, you can involve your audience more and increase its interest in your topic. At the beginning of your presentation, let people know when and how you are going to deal with any questions they may have. Audience participation usually increases the value of a presentation to everyone, but you need to make sure that people participate in a helpful way.

For example, you need to encourage discussions and questions while keeping people focused on relevant issues and keeping your eye on the clock.

Audience participation involves trying to get the audience to pay attention to the presentation and trying to get it to discuss any theories or issues that are raised. By encouraging audience participation, the audience becomes more active and engaged in the presentation, which can help make it more interesting.

Questions, as part of a presentation, are useful to

- encourage the audience to participate,
- encourage discussion,
- raise other useful information.

There are several methods you can use to encourage the audience to ask questions, after you have presented your business case:

try to give as many people as possible a chance to speak during discussions

If you notice one or two members of the audience dominating the discussion, you could say "You have made some interesting points, but let's bring others into the discussion."

ask open-ended questions to encourage discussion

To encourage discussion about a particular topic, ask the audience questions that are not answered with a simple "yes" or "no."

let people participate at their own comfort level

Some people are nervous or shy about giving their opinion in a group. Gently encourage participation by saying "I'm interested in what the rest of you think. Would anyone else like to comment?"

keep discussions on track

Ensure the discussion stays focused on the topic to avoid running over time or discussing irrelevant material. When the discussion switches to a different topic, tactfully bring it back on track by saying something like "That's interesting, but I'm not sure this is the right forum for that discussion."

don't let discussions go on for too long

Once you have made the point of your discussion clear, move on to the next part of the presentation to ensure you stay within the time allowed.

Anne is giving a presentation to the management of Blue Bay Software about the benefits of offering all employees free health insurance. Bill and Carrie are members of the audience. Follow along as Anne begins the questions and answers session of her presentation.

Anne: I'm interested to know what you all think about what I propose. Does anyone have any opinions?

Carrie: Well, I think it's a great idea. Health insurance can be very costly and it's reassuring to have it. I remember in the last company I worked in we had free health insurance. We also had paid sick leave, which really helped if you were sick for a few days. You never had to worry about it affecting your paycheck at the end of the month.

Anne: That's an interesting point, but let's stick with health insurance for the moment. What do you think, Bill? Do you think free health insurance is a good idea?

Bill: Um...yeah sure.

Anne: Does anyone else have any questions on this? If not, we can discuss other possible problems management may have in offering this to employees.

Anne used several methods to manage the question and answer session of her presentation.

She began by asking an open-ended question to the audience to encourage discussion. When the discussion was going off track, she brought it back to the topic of her presentation. However, she singled Bill out of the audience and asked him a closed-ended question. This resulted in Bill being forced to answer "yes". Also, he may not have been comfortable speaking in front of a group.

Then, Anne tried to encourage the rest of the audience to participate. She then moved the discussion along to another aspect of her presentation.

Question

Recognize methods of managing questions and answers after a business case presentation.

Options:

1. Try to give as many people as possible a chance to speak during discussions
2. Ask open-ended questions to encourage discussion
3. Allow the audience to give opinions for as long as it wants
4. Let people participate at their own comfort level
5. Pick out individuals from the audience to ask their opinion
6. Keep discussions on track
7. Don't let discussions go on for too long

Answer:

Option 1: This option is correct. Try to get everyone involved to avoid one or two members of the audience dominating the discussion.

Option 2: This option is correct. Open-ended questions encourage the audience to give its opinion, instead of answering questions with "yes" or "no."

Option 3: This option is incorrect. Once you have made your point, move on to the next part of the presentation to avoid running over time.

Option 4: This option is correct. Some people are nervous or shy about giving their opinion in a group.

Gently encourage audience participation, but do not force it.

Option 5: This option is incorrect. You should allow the audience to participate at their own comfort level. Some people might not like speaking up in a group.

Option 6: This option is correct. Keep the discussion to the point being made in the presentation to avoid running over time or discussing irrelevant material.

Option 7: This option is correct. Once you have made the point of your discussion clear, move on to the next part of the presentation to ensure you stay within the time allowed.

EFFECTIVELY CLOSE A PRESENTATION

Effectively close a presentation

The closing of your presentation is as important as the opening. You should always prepare a closing. Write down what you want to say so that you won't forget any important points. Closing a presentation helps you to summarize the important points of your presentation and refresh your audience's memory. When closing your presentation, you should:

restate your main point

At the beginning of your presentation, you told the audience what you were going to tell it. In your closing, you should restate what you told it.

say clearly what should happen next

It is important to tell the audience what it is supposed to do next or what is about to happen. Do not assume that it already know this.

call on the audience for action

If appropriate, tell your audience members what is required of them now, why they need to do something, and how to do it.

thank the audience

A presentation only takes place when there is an audience. Show your appreciation by thanking it sincerely for its attendance and attention.

Tom is a marketing executive with Aware Sportswear. He gives his department a presentation about the need for extra funding for advertising in order to increase sales.

He is now closing his presentation.

Tom: At the beginning of the presentation, I asked you how important you thought our advertising was and if you thought there was need for improvement.

When you look at the figures in the handout, it is clear that the company's sales will increase if we increase our advertising. I hope you now understand how important the extra funding is in order to achieve this.

Tom began the closing of his presentation by restating his main point, which was to gain extra funding. After restating his point, Tom continues with the closing of his presentation.

Tom: Tomorrow, I will send you all a summary of the main points of today's presentation, along with a sample budget. I would like you to review these items in preparation for next week.

Tom stated clearly what is going to happen next. This gives notice to the attendees that something is expected of them. It is important to do this; don't assume that people know this already. Tom proceeds to call his audience for action.

Tom: Next week, we need to discuss, as a team, how we are going to apply for extra funding. Everyone in the department will need to make a list of what extra materials they need and the estimated costs. We need to show the Finance department exactly what we need the money for.

Tom calls the audience to action by telling them what needs to be done, how to do it, and why it needs to be done. Finally, Tom finishes his presentation.

Tom: I'd like to thank you all for your time and attention. I know everyone is busy this time of year, and I really appreciate it.

Tom then finishes the presentation by thanking the audience sincerely.

Question

Which of the following are important points to consider when preparing a closing for your presentation?

Options:

1. Restate your main point
2. End the presentation with a question
3. Preparing a closing is unnecessary and time consuming
4. Say clearly what happens next
5. Call the audience for action
6. Thank the audience

Answer:

Option 1: This option is correct. It is important to summarize your presentation by reminding your audience of the main point.

Option 2: This option is incorrect. Ending a presentation with a question will only leave the audience confused.

Option 3: This option is incorrect. The closing is as important as the opening and should be prepared carefully.

Option 4: This option is correct. You need to tell the audience what is going to happen next. Don't assume that it will know this.

Option 5: This option is correct. You should tell the audience what needs to be done in order to achieve the objective of the presentation.

Option 6: This option is correct. Thank the audience sincerely to show that you appreciate its time and attention.

REFERENCES

References

- **Making Technology Investments Profitable: ROI Road Map to Better Business Cases** - 2003, Jack M. Keen, Bonnie Digrius, John Wiley & Sons
- **IT Investment: Making a Business Case** - 1999, Dan Remenyi, Butterworth-Heinemann (UK) MCIL
- **Persuasive Business Proposals: Writing to Win More Customers, Clients, and Contracts** - 2003, Tom Sant, AMACOM
- **Powerful Proposals: How to Give Your Business the Winning Edge** - 2005, David G. Pugh and Terry R. Bacon, AMACOM
- **IT Investment: Making a Business Case** - 1999, Dan Remenyi, Butterworth-Heinemann
- **Built to Learn: The Inside Story of How Rockwell Collins Became a True Learning Organization** - 2003, Cliff Purington, Chris Butler and Sarah Fister Gale, AMACOM

- **Practical Steps for Aligning Information Technology with Business Strategies: How to Achieve a Competitive Advantage** - 1994, Bernard H. Boar, John Wiley & Sons
- **Presentation Success: How to Plan, Prepare, and Deliver Effective Presentations** - 1999, Chan, Janis Fisher, AMACOM
- **Presentation Skills: A Practical Guide to Better Speaking, Third Edition** - 2000, Mandel, Steve, Crisp Learning
- **Technical Presentation Workbook: Winning Strategies for Effective Public Speaking, Second Edition** - 2002, Sullivan, Richard L. and Jerry L. Wircenski , ASME Press

GLOSSARY

Glossary

A

Anticipation of change - Expectation of, and preparation for, changes that may affect the new project. These include technology changes, social changes, and new projects introduced by rivals.

Appendix - A section of a Business case that contains all references, case studies, and testimonials that are referred to in the main body of the business case.

Assumptions - Assumptions are factors that are considered to be true, real, or certain for planning purposes.

B

Business case - A document containing information about a proposed project. It outlines the best way to deal with a problem or an opportunity that is facing a company.

Business case driver - A business factor that propels the need for the project now, rather than six months ago or six months from now.

Business concept - A concept that attempts to develop something new, something better, a new or under-served market, or greater integration of a company's products or services.

Business focus - Staying focused on the central character of the business to ensure that any new ideas that are developed are aligned with the corporate strategy.

C

Constraint - A restriction that will affect the performance of a project and limit activities throughout the project lifecycle.

Cost of capital - The rate of return that is necessary to make a project viable. This includes the interest rate, which is the cost of borrowing money, and the hurdle rate. This is the minimum return on investment that a new product must exceed.

Cost-benefit analysis - Analysis carried out to compare the costs and benefits of a project or activity.

Critical assumptions and constraints - A component of a business case that records critical assumptions and constraints made during the planning process.

Current inventory - The current inventory is all the finished products that are ready for sale, but haven't been sold yet.

D

Debt to asset ratio - The debt to asset ratio is calculated by dividing the company's total liabilities by the total assets.

Debt to worth ratio - The debt to worth ratio is calculated by dividing a company's total liabilities by the owners' equity (worth).

Decision criteria - The factors (both tangible and intangible) used by Decision makers to determine the attractiveness of investment alternatives.

Decision makers - The people in an organization who make investment decisions.

Discounted cash flow - The value of a future cash flow in terms of an equivalent value today. A future cash flow is discounted at some rate back to its present value so that all dollars, regardless of when collected, can be compared.

E

Economic life - The period of time during which an asset will have economic value and be usable.

Executive summary - A report on the organizational issues and outcomes of a Business case.

F

Fans - The Stakeholders who are actively in favor of the project, have an interest in the results, and are involved in the management of the changes brought about by the project.

Financial control - Establishing the profit margins for a project. This includes correctly estimating costs, such as research and marketing, having access to financial information, and managing cash flow.

Financial plan - Details of the benefit, cost, and risk analysis.

Financial ratios - Indicators of a firm's performance and financial situation. They are measures of capital, including debt to asset, current inventory, and debt to worth. They are derived from the information in a company's financial statements.

H

Hidden cost - An unseen Opportunity cost can become the hidden cost of that book of action. If there is no explicit monetary cost attached to a book of action, ignoring opportunity costs may produce the illusion that its benefits cost nothing at all.

I

In scope - An item that will be included in a project.

Industry health - The economic health of an industry is a strong indicator of whether a product will be successful. There is an increased chance that a new product or service will be successful if it responds to a healthy industry.

Intangible benefit - Benefits produced by an investment that are not immediately obvious and measurable.

Internal Rate of Return - The IRR is the interest rate that makes net present value of all cash flow equal to zero. This is the return that a company would earn if it expanded or invested in itself, rather than investing elsewhere.

IRR - See Internal Rate of Return

M

Main body - Describes the solution of the project.

Marginal costs - The costs of producing one more product or providing one more transaction.

Market factors - Key market factors that affect the product success include market readiness, demographics, the size of the market area, and pricing.

Mission statement - A concise description of the aim of a project.

N

Needs assessment - Contains the situational assessment or the problem statement. This should clearly establish the situation that currently exists that will be exploited or solved by the project. It should contain a description of the relevant environmental conditions, an assessment of how the business needs are currently being met, or not met, or an analysis of the gap between the current situation and the stated objectives.

Net Present Value - Often abbreviated to NPV. Used to calculate and analyze the profitability of a project. The present value of cash inflows is subtracted from the present value of cash outflows.

NPV compares the value of a sum of money today versus the value of that same sum of money in the future, after taking inflation and return into account. If the NPV of a prospective project is positive, then it should be accepted. If it is negative, then the project should be rejected.

NPV - See Net Present Value

O

Objective - Describes clearly and precisely what a project is expected to deliver.

Old defenders - The Stakeholders who will actively resist a project because they see it as a threat to their current position.

Opportunity cost - The cost of something in terms of an untaken opportunity (and the benefits that could be received from that opportunity) or the most valuable alternative.

Out of scope - Something that will not be included in a project.

P

Presentation strategy - The approach used to persuade decision makers of the attractiveness of an investment option when presenting a business case.

Project management - A project is more likely to succeed if the managers possess certain attributes: industry or management experience, a realistic approach to business needs, a flexible attitude to change, and the ability to work well with other people.

Project team - A list of the people who will be responsible for implementing the project, and contains relevant information about the team members.

Project work plan - See Work plan

Purpose of the business statement - A component of a business case that describes the problem or opportunity that the project will address.

Q

Quantifiable benefit - A benefit that can be measured.

R

ROI - Acronym for Return on Investment. The ROI is the ratio of net benefits to costs. The formula is benefits minus costs divided by costs.

S

Scope - Defines the boundaries of a proposed project and states them clearly for the audience and decision makers. The scope defines the size of a project. Scope can include such areas as project deliverables, schedule, features, functions, team, resources, and standards and guidelines.

Silent partners - The Stakeholders who are in favor of a project but play a passive role in the project development and thus have no real influence on the project at all.

Situational assessment and problem statement - Establishes the benefit to the organization for proceeding with the project.

Sleeping dogs - The Stakeholders who are not in favor of a project but play a passive role in the project development and thus have no real influence on the project at all.

SMART - Acronym for Specific, Measurable, Achievable, Realistic, and Timely. Often applied to an Objective.

Stakeholders - Any group or organization that a business impacts upon or interacts with and can influence the long-term success of that business.

T

Table of contents - A list of the major headings in a business case and the page on which each is found.

Tangible benefit - A benefit produced by an investment that is immediately obvious and measurable.

Technical analysis - Provides a more detailed technical analysis of the implications of the situational assessment and problem statement.

Terminal value - The value of an investment at the end of a period, taking into account a specified rate of interest. It is the value of a fully depreciated asset, such as a car or a computer at the end of its life.

Time value of money - The value derived from the use of money over time. The present value is the value today of an amount that would exist in the future with a stated investment rate. Future value is the value in the future of a known amount today with a stated investment rate.

Title page - A page containing the title of a Business case.

U

Unquantifiable benefit - A benefit that cannot be measured.

W

Work plan - A document that shows an overall path for the development of a project and what is necessary to achieve it.

Printed in Great Britain
by Amazon